33 Ways to Become a Better Recruiter
(and Human)

Kieran O'Connor

Kieran's an expert of his craft and his experiences shine through in this practical guide to recruitment. Packed with actionable tips, the book empowers readers to make a positive impact. But it's not all cold hard skills; Kieran emphasises the human side of recruitment, offering valuable advice on building strong candidate relationships. 33 Ways to Become a Better Recruiter (and Human) is a great resource for anyone starting out, and for those looking for a refresher and wanting to elevate their recruitment game.

Nigel Doughty, Chief Operating Officer

As someone who's worked in recruitment and other industries, I found this book to be an invaluable resource filled with actionable insights and practical tips. This book is a treasure trove of lessons for anyone with a growth mindset looking to enhance their recruitment skills, providing strategies to continually learn and improve. It's the book I wish I had read when I began my journey in recruitment.

Kieran's values shine through every chapter of this book. His commitment to continuous learning, integrity, and building strong relationships is seamlessly woven into the fabric of this book.

Whether you're a novice or a seasoned professional, the lessons within will help you refine your skills and develop a mindset geared towards excellence. This book is not just about recruitment; it's about becoming the best version of yourself!

Alex Kavel, Product Manager, Co-organiser of ProductTank and ex-Talent Acquisition Manager

It's fair to say that I've had a mixed experience with recruiters over the years; however, Kieran has taken the time to understand our business and the people that fit our culture. He works tirelessly to find the right person for the role, while keeping both

parties updated throughout the process. I would highly recommend Kieran!
Will Roberts, Managing Director

Kieran is one of the good recruiters,. As a candidate he's thoroughly listened to the requirements I've set out and has kept regular contact to keep me informed on the current state of the market and any opportunities which might be worth discussing – even at the peril of his commission at times! He's easy to work with, doesn't badger me and makes the process easy.

On the other side, as a recruiting manager I've had a number of great candidates from him, again listening to the requirements of the role and delivering. He's my go to for anything recruitment related.
Mark Rawson, Chief Technology Officer

Kieran is an outstanding recruiter who excels in building relationships and getting a thorough understanding of client needs through a consultative approach. I've worked with Kieran for the last eighteen months and see him as my go to recruiter for any roles and also for an honest and pragmatic view of the market. On the candidate side, all of Kieran's candidates are fully matched, qualified and prepared for interview, which has made my life easier knowing that he has a high standard when representing candidates.
Leroy Brito, Talent Acquisition Manager and Comedian

Kieran is one of our trusted recruitment partners, having worked closely together on 'hard to fill roles' over the last two years. Kieran has a great understanding of our company culture, the skills we require in our teams and has successfully placed many candidates for us.

Kieran has done a great job at finding candidates for us (which

is no easy feat!!!), working in both a challenging market and with a niche talent pool within the South Wales region.
Sharna Picken, People Manager

Kieran has helped us find a number of great tech candidates when we were struggling to find them via other sources. We particularly appreciate how Kieran is truly focused on the needs of our business, and the specific person and role specification, tailoring his advice to us. He has provided pertinent and valuable input when we have needed it, and has a detailed knowledge of the tech space.

In addition, Kieran is great to work with. He is incredibly responsive, but also respects and understands that we have a business to run, and balances well the essential need to communicate with a recognition that we are all busy! Put simply, I have never felt 'chased' by Kieran, only supported to achieve our recruitment goals. I would highly recommend Kieran.
Steve Brind, Head of Product Development

Kieran is a rare find and one of the good guys. Focused, disciplined and driven, with bags of perseverance. He exhibits these qualities in and out of work and the results speak for themselves.

Kieran was a pleasure to manage. He was extremely conscientious and always brought his A game. Of equal importance, his moral compass was always on point with an ethical, fair and professional approach to all situations.

On a personal note he was a pleasure to work with and a really nice guy. Impeccably dressed, polite and humble.

I'd highly recommend Kieran to anyone. Clients, candidates and colleagues."
Simon Girling, Managing Director

Being a young, early-stage founder, the thought of recruiting for your company can be a scary thing. There's a lot of ways to recruit, a lot of strategies to explore around interviewing and decision-making, and often knowing where to even start is difficult.

Kieran's approach to recruitment is refreshing – a no nonsense approach that truly takes the needs of the business into account. He knows the recruitment world inside and out and will offer all the advice you need by referencing past experiences and major wins for similar businesses.

I have read a lot of books about business and recruitment, but knowing the author of this great book, I can safely say that every piece of advice and guidance is authentic! It's a great resource for anyone starting their journey in understanding how to recruit for your business.

Ieuan Leigh, Chief Executive Officer

Kieran is a rare find. One of the handful of recruiters I've met in my time that I respect and trust.

Being someone who has run the technology operations for several small and large businesses, a recruitment relationship with an external agency is something that I put high value on.

Kieran is nothing short of an expert communicator. He listens, he advises and most importantly, he delivers on his word. I recommend this book to anyone looking to improve the way they recruit."

Andy Jones, Chief Technology Officer

The right of Kieran O'Connor to be identified as the Author of the Work has been asserted by him in accordance with the Copyright, Designs and Patents Act 1988.

Editorial, interior design and typesetting: Will Rees
Cover design: Lewis Quinney
ISBN: 978-1-917022-43-9

Printed and bound in the UK by
4edge, 22 Eldon Way, Hockley, Essex, SS5 4AD

Published by
Jelly Bean Books
Mackintosh House
136 Newport Road, Cardiff, CF24 1DJ
www.candyjarbooks.co.uk

All rights reserved. No part of this publication may be reproduced, stored in a retrieval system, or transmitted at any time or by any means, electronic, mechanical, photocopying, recording or otherwise without the prior permission of the copyright holder. This book is sold subject to the condition that it shall not by way of trade or otherwise be circulated without the publisher's prior consent in any form of binding or cover other than that in which it is published.

Contents

Introduction	**1**
Tip One	
If You Can Become Anything, Become Coachable	**6**
Tip Two	
Under Promise and Overdeliver	**10**
Tip Three	
Influence Your Meeting Outcomes by Following Up	**14**
Tip Four	
Don't Open an Email or Message Until You're Ready to Respond to It	**18**
Tip Five	
Have a Healthy Lunch	**23**
Tip Six	
Everyone Wants a Hollywood Star	**28**
Tip Seven	
Turn Up Fifteen Minutes Early Everywhere You Go	**32**
Tip Eight	
Dress for the Day You Want to Have	**36**

Tip Nine
Master Your Pre-Meeting Rituals — **40**

Tip Ten
Prioritise Lead Generation Everyday — **44**

Tip Eleven
No Update Is Still an Update — **48**

Tip Twelve
Invest in a Diary and Plan Your Days — **53**

Tip Thirteen
Get Face Time with Your Clients — **57**

Tip Fourteen
Study Your Competition — **61**

Tip Fifteen
Get Specific with Your Calling Times — **65**

Tip Sixteen
Develop a Growth Mindset Over a Fixed One — **69**

Tip Seventeen
Invest in Your Own Personal Development — **73**

Tip Eighteen
Make Networking a Priority — **77**

Tip Nineteen
Always Provide Value, Don't Be a Vulture — **81**

Tip Twenty
Get Good at Writing Job Adverts — **86**

Tip Twenty-One
Physical Health Will Get You to the Top and Keep You There — **91**

Tip Twenty-Two
Take Your Mental Health Seriously — **95**

Tip Twenty-Three
Asking Better Questions Produces Better Answers — **99**

Tip Twenty-Four
Build Your Personal Brand Online | **103**
Tip Twenty-Five
Strengthen Your Reputation and Protect It at All Costs | **108**
Tip Twenty-Six
Hold Yourself Accountable, to Everything | **112**
Tip Twenty-Seven
Talk Less, Listen More | **116**
Tip Twenty-Eight
Don't Just Deliver, Trial Close | **120**
Tip Twenty-Nine
Be Caring and Kind | **125**
Tip Thirty
Be Humble with Your Victories and Gracious in Your Defeats | **129**
Tip Thirty-One
The Money Is in the Follow Up | **133**
Tip Thirty-Two
Aspire to Become a True Consultant | **136**
Tip Thirty-Three
Proactivity Beats Reactivity, Every Time | **140**

Conclusion | **144**

Introduction

Recruitment is well on its way to being a respected industry, an industry that, if you apply yourself and are fully committed to your own development, can provide a prosperous, lifelong career. It might not yet have the respect of law, finance or accounting (my assumption is that it's because there's an element of sales involved, and we know what most people think of salespeople), but recruitment is one of the few industries that will enhance your life skills at the same time as your professional career. Two of the most important skills in life are the ability to sell, not just a product but yourself, and the capability of building strong relationships. Both of these skills are at the heart of recruitment, and if you can hone them, you're likely to flourish.

We as professionals still have a lot of work to do with

improving the industry, though. I imagine most of you reading this will already be working in recruitment, and a large percentage early on in your recruitment careers. If you haven't found out already, I think it's only right of me to share how challenging this industry can be. According to multiple surveys throughout 2023, there are approximately 30,000 recruitment agencies in operation, and over 200,000 individual people working in the industry. That's *a lot* of competition.

But let's not forget that the recruitment industry contributes an estimated £40billion – yes, that's billions, not millions – to the UK economy per year. Some quick maths shows a yearly market share of £200,000 for every single person in the industry.

I know what you're thinking: I'd take a £200k salary, no problem; just give me a phone and I'll start calling. Sadly for us, it doesn't work like that. The competition is fierce and there are many recruiters that eat up more than their market share.

A £200,000 biller used to be the epitome of a competent recruiter – a recruiter to be respected and admired. And don't get me wrong: I do consider £200,000 billings to be good. But there are recruiters out there who would say otherwise. In some agencies, there are high performers who have perfected their craft and can personally contribute half a million, or even a million pounds of revenue through one desk. Permanent recruiters who are operating in niche markets, some in Europe and the USA, can bill between £200,000 and £700,000.

Yes, the million-pound billers will almost certainly be running a contract desk, and if you work in the permanent world, you'll likely contribute far less than this. The point I'm trying to make is, if you're going to choose recruitment as a career, you need to dream bigger than you are right now. The opportunities that will be presented to you along your journey will surprise you.

For those not driven by money, there are many recruitment roles that aren't as high-intensity or mentally demanding as the 360 agency recruiter role, and they still pay fairly well. But if you're signing up to be a 360 external recruiter, you'd best be in it for the money, at least partially. You can still help people; that's what recruiting is all about. But this world can be gruelling.

Whilst I'm a passionate external recruiter, the concepts shared in this book are for anyone who's involved in the recruitment industry. This book contains a cornucopia of tips to help anyone in the world of recruitment, whether you are an in-house, external, freelance – however you've positioned your career. When I refer to the 'client', this can be understood as either an external company you are supporting as an agency, or an internal stakeholder you service as an in-house.

Recruitment can be a tough place, and I'm sure we can all agree there is sometimes an invisible war between in-house and external. Both often assume the other knows how to navigate the process, and sadly both often think they're more in control than the other. I imagine a future where all recruiters are aligned in achieving the same goals and adhering to best practices, and that will come when all recruiters respect each other regardless of their position in the industry.

The concepts in this book can, and should, be considered by anyone, regardless of any protected characteristics or length of time in recruitment. In this modern world of recruitment, a Gen Z can join an established company and on day one utilise a technology stack that allows them to sell and compete all over the world. Using just a mobile phone, they can have access to their CRM, job boards, LinkedIn, LinkedIn Recruiter, SourceBreaker, Slack... The tools and technology available to recruiters right now make it one of the most interesting times in history to be a part of this thriving industry.

But when it comes to recruitment and tech, let's address the elephant in the room: artificial intelligence. AI won't take a recruiter's job in the next few years. Not even in the next decade. What AI will do is allow you to automate certain parts of your role, the boring parts, allowing you to increase your speed and efficiency. If used correctly, it will no doubt propel you to a new level. Here's the thing: recruiters can be so caught up in our technology-driven world that they forget the fundamentals of recruitment. The core basics of human interaction. AI can't read body language, pick up on cues, listen for prompts or read emotion in people's eyes (yet). That's why I've invested time into this book, to support and hopefully inspire you to be the best recruiter, and human, you can be. You see, this book is a mix of tips and tricks related to recruiting, but also to personality skills and attributes that transcend the industry.

Your life, both personal and professional, is made up of small things. Lots of small things. When we look back over the years, it's rare to see one monumental situation that completely changed our trajectory, but hundreds if not thousands of micro decisions compounded over time. A new habit we implemented. A new set of standards we decided to live by. Over time, your small changes amalgamate and you're operating as a new person.

I truly hope you enjoy reading this book as much as I've

enjoyed writing it. Like with most personal development books, there's a high chance you'll already be working on some of these areas, and I encourage you to continue that journey. There may be areas that, with some thinking, you realise you may need to address and improve on. This isn't a book that will turn you into a high-performance machine simply by skimming all thirty-three tips; I encourage you to read through and digest each tip in detail. You're welcome to make notes and expand on some of the points I've shared. But most importantly keep in mind that, at the end of the day, recruiting is about other people: supporting others to become better versions of themselves. I wish you nothing but success.

Tip One

If You Can Become Anything, Become Coachable

*'My best skill was that I was coachable.
I was a sponge and aggressive to learn.'*
Michael Jordan, American businessman
and former NBA Allstar

If Michael Jordan says that his best skill was his coachability, I think we all can and should take a leaf out of his incredible book. Coachability is a trait that needs to be developed in us all; I don't believe it comes naturally to many. As humans, we have built-in egos and a real sense of pride, and that pride can feel challenged when we're given constructive feedback, particularly if it goes against our core values or the identity we have assigned ourselves. From my perspective, coachability is how willing a person is to hold themselves accountable for their own actions and development. Not only that, but how accepting they are of feedback, and more importantly, how they will use that feedback moving forward.

If You Can Become Anything, Become Coachable | 7

I'm not sure why there is such a lot of ego in the recruitment world (the low barrier to entry and the outsized financial returns perhaps) but all too often ego gets in the way of becoming coachable. Some time ago, I read a fantastic book called *Get Out of Your Own Way*, by Mark Goulston and Philip Gouldberg. A lot of the concepts in that book resonate with the idea of coachability, but one quote really stuck with me: 'You can't fix something until you admit it's broken.' I think the word 'admit' stands out to me here. It can feel physically and mentally challenging to admit to yourself that something you're doing isn't working or isn't producing the best results; it can be difficult to let yourself be open to a new way of thinking. It takes time and conscious effort.

As Greg Savage, the author and worldwide recruitment rockstar, says in his book *The Savage Way*, recruitment isn't rocket science after all, how hard can it be? I truly think this has an effect on recruiters' willingness to be coached, particularly as they progress through the ranks and earn their stripes. All we're really doing is speaking to people and placing them into new business, what more can I be taught? Whilst recruitment isn't rocket science, the truth is, not many industries are. Yet despite most business owners, founders or executive teams thinking they have the time and skills to handle their own recruiting, many of you reading will know from experience that this is often not the case.

It is these individuals, high-ranking and adept in their own industries, who all too often are unwilling to be coached: on what the most effective recruiting process might look like; on how quickly they may need to move to secure the best talent; who, worst of all, will low ball the perfect candidate and blow the opportunity to pick up the perfect talent (no matter how much free fruit is available in the office).

This lack of coachability in clients and even colleagues can be frustrating at times, but it's out of our control. What we can control is our awareness that becoming coachable is an important part of recruitment, and life in general, that will greatly expedite our own personal development journey.

From the perspective of someone just starting out in recruitment, maybe in your first year or two, please don't let your wins expand your head too quickly. Acknowledge and celebrate them, let them spur you on to more success, but always remember, there will be bumps along the road. As Michael Jordan so eloquently put it, he was 'a sponge and aggressive to learn'. A sponge is exactly what you want to be: someone who is constantly absorbing knowledge, tips and advice from people you look up to and respect. By positioning yourself as someone who is eager to learn, and putting yourself in the same rooms as people you aspire to, you're building your subconscious mind to think and behave differently, simply by being there. Your conscious mind will pick up on new skills of ways of thinking, but it's the unconscious mind that needs to be developed, too.

You might be reading this five, seven, ten or even twenty years into your recruitment prison stretch - erm, I mean career - and you may well be right if thinking you know most of what recruitment involves. Although the tech and tools available to us are developing by the day, the core principles of recruitment haven't changed drastically over the years. But no matter how much you do know, there is always someone who knows something or someone you don't - always. No matter how deep you are into your career, there are people who can sharpen your

If You Can Become Anything, Become Coachable

thinking and expose you to new methods, areas or opportunities. These conversations will sometimes be difficult, but as the wise business professional and author Kenneth H. Blanchard quoted, 'When you stop learning you stop growing.'

Some of you might be wondering how you exhibit to others that you are willing to be coached. From experience, being coachable is something that you have to consciously decide to make a part of your identity. Determine to be open-minded and to listen to other people's advice and criticism, and to project this attitude so that others recognise it. A sense of curiosity will make your coach feel like you're invested. Never be afraid to ask questions that start with why, how or what.

The salient point is that you have to turn up with the right attitude, every day. When it's time for you to attend training or a workshop, when it's time for you to have a one-on-one with your manager, and when you get to speak to anyone with more experience in your field than you, make sure you're applying the right attitude. For me, that attitude should be one of willingness to listen and a desire to learn.

Tip Two
Under Promise and Overdeliver

'The formula for success: under promise and over deliver.'
Tom Peters, American writer and author

The recruitment industry is built on expectations. The clients we choose to work with have expectations of recruiters providing access to a specific type of person and skillset within a certain timeframe. The candidates we represent have expectations of honest advice, regular communication and ultimately a guided entrance into companies that they may not otherwise get contact with. And let's not forget, we all have either managers, business owners, stakeholders or investors who are expecting us to be held accountable to our own words, forecasts and predictions.

With all this weight on our shoulders, it makes me wonder why so many of us make life difficult for ourselves by over-promising. I would go so far as to say it's one of the biggest downfalls that we create for ourselves as an industry. You could say that it comes down to lack of experience and

Under Promise and Overdeliver | 11

recruiters not being close enough to the changes and expectations of their market. You could also suggest a trend between excitement and setting unrealistic expectations – being so caught up in speaking to that unicorn candidate, or receiving a new job, that you simply tell people what they want to hear, rather than what they need to hear. Or, depending on how deeply you want to think about it, it could come down to an underlying sense of wanting to be liked, being a yes person and not having the confidence to have a challenging conversation.

Either way, by setting unrealistic expectations, we are setting ourselves up for failure.

Let's look at it from the perspective of a client. Our services are not cheap, so when a company chooses to use us, it's because they want a quicker route to market and direct access to our talent pools, saving their own time. Knowing the importance of speed of results, it's crucial we make the client aware of the worst-case scenario. Let's say that you know a search for a certain scarce skillset will without a doubt take two weeks at best. Depending on the time of year, the salary you are working with and a few other variables, that could easily become a four-week search. This fact, however unwelcome, needs to be communicated to the client: it is the first step in their developing a clear understanding of what goes on in our world. From communicating the length of time a search might take, should follow an explanation why: why the desired skillset isn't common, what the next five-to-seven days will involve, when they can expect to receive CVs, how likely it is that they'll see someone who ticks all the boxes...

Now from the candidate's perspective. Here we should be as honest as possible. It's no secret that it can sometimes feel awkward telling a candidate they aren't skilled enough for the role, that you don't feel like it's best practice to share their CV for a particular position. But generally people will respect you for your integrity. When we work in partnership with a candidate on a job search, we're working as a team, and if both parties can communicate openly and honestly, the team will be stronger for it. There will be times when you share a candidate's profile with a client and receiving feedback might take five days. Why not let them know this in the first conversation, rather than saying, 'We'll be in touch soon'?

Next we come to setting expectations for whoever we report to, whether a manager, a director, a business owner or an investor. This is perhaps the one area where people – and not just recruiters – let themselves down the most. The people we report to will have their own goals, targets and milestones to hit, so they'll likely expect to hear words that support those measurements. Let's imagine we have a £10,000 target for the month, and we need to forecast to a manager what placements we're expecting to secure; naturally it feels right to accumulate as much information as possible, sometimes even fabricating the chances of a placement to keep them satisfied. The problem is, if we forecast £10,000 with two placements, and that's literally all the possibilities we have for that month, not only are we going to be held accountable to our words, but we haven't left any room to overdeliver. On the contrary, if we have the same target of £10,000, but have the chance of securing four placements, would it not make sense to share our two that have the best chances, and to leave the other two as an unexpected bonus?

What we should never do, as humans or recruiters, is outright lie, nor withhold any information that we would be

Under Promise and Overdeliver | 13

expected to share. However, there is a fine art and a key difference between oversharing and ultimately underdelivering on agreed expectations, compared to under promising and overdelivering. To have the self-awareness to under promise may take time and may not feel natural at first, like most other tips in this book. When dealing with clients and candidates, the ability to quickly assess specific timescales and expectations will be invaluable; then, once these are calculated, quickly figuring on the margins to overdeliver.

The next time you are to meet with your manager to discuss your weekly or monthly goals, take your time and remember that whoever holds the most information usually has an advantage. Again, I do not encourage lying, nor have I ever lied in any of my forecasting sessions. What I *have* done is commit only to goals, targets or deals that I was almost certain would be achievable. You may have plenty of extra information to share, and it may feel uncomfortable withholding information from your manager, but sometimes it's necessary. I can assure you that there is no quicker way to burden your reputation as a recruiter than to regularly fall short of your agreed targets. Whether it's with clients, candidates, colleagues or managers, we must leave room to overdeliver, and we do that by purposely setting expectations lower than we perceive our prospects to be.

Tip Three
Influence Your Meeting Outcomes by Following Up

'Respect is a two-way street;
if you want to get it, you've got to give it.'
Mandy Rose, American professional wrestler
and television personality

Have you ever had a meeting that went so well that you couldn't wait to get back to the office to tell everyone? You know the one: there was an instant connection between you and the prospect, the communication was effortless, and you may have even picked up some new business to work on immediately. Result! You've been holding in your inner salesperson the whole meeting, but mentally you've already spent that commission. Four new tops from your favourite brand, a dinner date at high-end restaurant, and that's the next six months' Huel subscription sorted.

    A successful meeting is an incredible feeling and should be enjoyed for as long as you feel necessary. Some of us like

Influence Your Meeting Outcomes by Following Up | 15

to text a friend or partner, some prefer to buy themselves a coffee, and almost everyone enjoys telling the rest of the office just how good we were. But there can be a negative outcome from all this excitement, and that's a lack of conviction post-interview. Some of you might think that, at this point, the job is done, but I disagree.

This tip here is to remind you, or even introduce you to why and how we should create an effective meeting follow up. As (generally speaking) the organiser of the meeting, it is absolutely essential we're the first to follow up. The difference between whether we or the prospect follow up first may seem miniscule, but there's a common theme throughout this book, and it's that we should consistently construct a positive, professional mental image of ourselves in our prospects. In an ideal world, we want to be the first to show our appreciation to the other party, to demonstrate our attentiveness by exquisitely relaying key parts of our conversation, to express our gratitude for their time and meticulously explain our next steps.

A lot of information can be shared in a meeting, and most of it will be new and important; a quick recap can help both parties retain as much information as possible. It also allows us to demonstrate our consistency by beginning to deliver what we promised during the meeting, whether a referral, a quick turnaround in terms of business, or some candidate profiles. Once the meeting is over, the question for our prospects becomes if and how we follow through on our promises. Anything that we assure a prospect we can or will do should be done as a high priority, and a follow up affords the first opportunity to get the ball rolling.

The quintessential analogy I used to share with team members was to think about your favourite sandwich. The foundation of a good sandwich is of course how you start it, the first slice of bread. This is your opening line, and if you don't get this right, your email is going to fall apart. The opening line should express some gratitude and maybe some light humour, depending on how well the conversation went. This, for me, is the sourdough of openings – simply the best, I hope you'd agree.

But as we all know, the most important part of any sandwich is the fillings you choose. That may be salad, meat, veg or meat substitutes, depending on your diet, but it all comes down to the right ingredients in the right combination. The information we include in the next two to four lines determines a lot. It is important to demonstrate how well we listened in the meeting, that we truly understand the problems the prospect is facing. Generally, your email should include specific information that's relevant to your service or offering, areas such as how many hires they plan to make over the next twelve months, current problems within the workforce, new budgets being allocated for recruitment or other activities, a new senior individual joining the team. Something personal, like their favourite sports team or a hobby they mentioned, typically also goes down well, and the more specific you can be with numbers or dates, the better. Everyone loves to feel heard, so it's important you truly listen to understand the prospect's world, not just to reply to their comments. This is where we can stand out from the rest of the crowd.

I'm sure I don't need to explain to anyone that, to complete a sandwich, you need a final piece of bread. Whilst it's the last ingredient, you simply don't have a proper sandwich without it. Our final line, similar to the first, should be fairly short and sweet, signing off and alluding to next steps or agreed timelines. This may look different every time, but often it will involve sharing excitement for the next time you plan to meet, and giving an agreed date for when they will hear from you next. Again, the more specific and the more personable, the better.

This tip can and should be followed after any meeting, whether it be with a prospect, new or existing business, an external supplier or even a candidate. I've crossed paths with many people inside and outside of recruitment who fall guilty of not following up on promises or referrals. I appreciate conversation will flow and light comments be exchanged, but our words are compelling, so if we promise to introduce someone to someone, or share a document with them, we should make sure that's done within the hour. This is simply non-negotiable. Think about a time where someone you've met has told you they'll do something, usually something that would really add value to you, then they don't. You either need to reluctantly follow up with them or let it slide, but either way your expectations of that person have now dropped. If they can't follow up on the most basic of promises, how can you trustingly do business with this person?

The primary goal of our post-meeting follow up is to build our credibility with the prospect, by showing that we've digested and retained key information. We want to create the impression that we care, are a professional in our industry and an expert communicator. Everyone wants to be heard, and prospects are no different to anyone else, although we may treat them that way sometimes. It's the small details that really make a difference to the perception we create of ourselves in other people.

Tip Four
Don't Open an Email or Message Until You're Ready to Respond to It

'The single biggest problem in communication is the illusion that it has taken place.'
George Bernard Shaw, Irish playwright and critic

There has never been a time in history like we are experiencing now. We are able to connect with almost anyone worldwide at the click of a button. Whilst our ancestors would consider this a luxury, along with it comes enormous pressure. Our mental capacity is stretched like never before, with a lot of us experiencing information overload. Various studies have been done on this concept, which refers to when the amount of information exceeds the working memory of the person receiving it. For centuries, each generation has had to take in new sources of information: newspapers, which are thought to have been around since the 1600s, radios in the 1920s, television in the '50s, the traditional PC in the '70s and mobile phones in the '80s. And in the modern day, now there's the smartphone.

Don't Open an Email Until You're Ready to Respond | 19

All these sources scrap for our attention every hour; if we put down the laptop we'll pick up our smartphone; if we're not on our smartphone we're usually watching another screen, most likely the TV.

Let's bring this back to recruitment, where most of our responsibilities are communication-based, whether that be emails, calls, LinkedIn or text messages. Some of us experience an overwhelming amount of messages and emails, well into the 100s per day. With our attention being pulled from left to right by an endless amount of notifications, how can we really ensure we're effectively responding to all of our messages?

Thinking back to the beginning of my recruitment career, I realise that I unknowingly picked up some not so positive habits, which I'm sure some of you fall guilty of too. Let's imagine you're in the middle of some deep work, a real flow of concentration, and you see that email pop up in the bottom corner of your screen, or a notification on your phone. It's from a client. What do most of us think? We must act now. Let me just see what it says. Maybe it's life or death (it never is).

There are a few reasons why our curiosity in such instances doesn't benefit us. Think of those times you're switching between tasks, and it becomes a real challenge to gain momentum. Multiple studies have presented information that shows that, when we are distracted from a flow state in one task, it can take twenty-three minutes to regain that concentration and momentum. Now, add up all the distractions we encounter throughout our day, and it's no wonder why some days we feel like we've not really accomplished anything substantial.

Another example: I'm a big fan of networking events, and I'll usually attend one or two weekly. There have been times when I've been in a positive mood with my conversations flowing nicely, but I decide to check my emails, knowing full well I'm not in a place to reply. Often, amongst the positive emails, there have been some negative updates that have ruined my mood. This simply would not have happened if I had waited until I was in a position to read, digest and respond to them correctly. Protect your energy and mood at all costs, particularly when in front of prospects and clients, and schedule some time to respond to messages when you have full mental capacity.

One of the worst things a recruiter can do, in my view, is to open an email or message, read it, and decide to reply later. We know that's a lie we have told ourselves, and there's a high chance we'll forget to reply within a reasonable timeframe. We're supposed to be super-communicators, yet all too often we open communications by snubbing the other party.

How many times have you, or people you're in contact with, had to apologise for opening the message, saying you 'thought you replied'? We've all done it. Most of the time we reply mentally but decide to park it to the side to eat lunch, hoping to reply when we've got more mental capacity. Do we reply after? More than likely not. If you're anything like me, often it's not until three days pass, and it's 6:10pm, and you're cooking dinner with your partner and all of a sudden it hits you: damn! I haven't replied to so and so. Now you have to face the awkwardness of explaining that you're very sorry, you thought you'd got back to them, etcetera etcetera. But the damage is already done.

There has to be a better way, right? After putting some thought into it, I've chosen to work with a framework. I have

Don't Open an Email Until You're Ready to Respond | 21

time blocks throughout my working day when I simply do not monitor my phone notifications or have email pop ups. These blocks are usually an hour, sometimes ninety minutes, and are reserved for the most important tasks of the day, usually business development and candidate work (sourcing for a specific role or lead generation). Outside of these time blocks, I reserve thirty minutes at the end of my day to complete all of my communication admin tasks, like replying to LinkedIn messages or important emails.

The best recruiters out there are proactive rather than reactive, but there's no getting away from the fact that a huge part of the recruitment game is reacting swiftly. If I'm working outside of my core time blocks, it's usually on something that doesn't need a deep flow state of work, so I'm content to open emails and notifications when they come in. A non-negotiable for me, and something I would encourage you to pick up, is that if I'm able to reply to that message within two minutes, I reply immediately. Sure, there may be times when you'll have a client ask you to arrange an interview and you need to contact someone before replying, or a candidate asks you to check a timesheet; but even then I'll take action immediately. I think us recruiters have a strange conception that replying to emails and messages too fast makes it seem like we're not busy, or like we're overly keen. Whilst I can understand the thought process, I disagree. I've replied to emails the same minute they come through, I've replied to LinkedIn sales outreach within minutes and I've replied to texts from candidates with a returned phone call the second they come through.

The results? Your productivity goes through the roof, and the communication between your clients and candidates improves. By communicating more efficiently, you can shave hours and days from your workflows. But you can only do so if you reply when you're ready to reply. In other words, when all of your other work is squared away.

Tip Five
Have a Healthy Lunch

'Your diet is a bank account.
Good food choices are good investments.'
Bethenny Frankel, American TV personality and philanthropist

Whether or not we enjoy the process of making and eating food, it's something we must do every single day, for the rest of our lives. From my perspective, if we indisputably need to eat food to survive, why don't we at least try to learn to enjoy the process? Wouldn't it be beneficial to understand the benefits of different types of food, and rather than eating to survive, eating to fuel our bodies and minds?

Changing our mentality around food, what it does to our body and how we can maximise our energy output with the foods we eat, takes time and discipline. As many of us will know, with recruitment being primarily an office- or at least seated-based role, before you know it, unhealthy eating habits can really take a toll on our physical health.

Recruitment is a popular career path with people who did

and maybe still do play sports to a good, sometimes even semi-professional level. I'm generalising here, and speaking to males as a male, but our younger bodies may have been used to a high calorie diet with vigorous exercise multiple times a week. As we progress through our recruitment careers, climbing the ladder of progression, it's when these sporting activities stop that we notice a huge decline in our physical health. The recruitment belly, dare I say. For my female audience, on the other hand, I can't comment for you obviously; I'm sure you all look great. In all seriousness, from my experience at least, women seem to handle the transition through recruitment with grace. The same can't be said for us men.

Recruitment can be known for its long days, most of which are spent sitting down at a desk, in front of a screen. Whilst recruitment, and most other office jobs for that matter, aren't physically demanding, it certainly requires a lot of mental energy. You're probably familiar with the term metabolism, the process by which our body changes food and drink into energy. In simple terms, when we eat food, our body will break down the macronutrients and transport these nutrients throughout the body, usually via the bloodstream. You might be in the mindset that physical work is the only way you can burn calories, but that's where you're wrong. While the brain represents just 2% of a typical person's total body weight, it accounts for 20% of the body's energy use, and requires approximately 500 calories per day. How many calories are in the average person's lunch? 400-700, and a minimum of 20% of that is distributed to the brain as an immediate priority.

Although some of us may be aware of just how important it is to eat healthy, anyone who's worked in recruitment for

Have a Healthy Lunch | 25

longer than six months will agree that some days are so uncontrollably busy that it is hard to prioritise. Let's be real, in the modern world, it's far more convenient to order a Subway or McDonalds via Deliveroo, or join the team's order for a Domino's, than to a prep a meal the night before or walk fifteen minutes to a healthy salad bar.

The commitment to healthy eating requires a lot of effort when starting out, and it can be challenging to find the time, and let's not forget, sometimes expensive. But physical health is the foundation of everything, and that includes achieving high performance in our career. By simply choosing to eat well and adopt a healthy lifestyle, we're well on the way to improving almost all areas of our life.

Once you have the habits and structure in place for healthy eating, other areas slip into place. There are four main areas of health – physical, spiritual, financial and mental – and physical health is the support structure for them all. Think about it: eating right will make us feel and look better, increasing our energy and our mood, which will in turn allow us to perform better and for longer in the three other areas. Do we really think anyone wants to go to yoga in the evening after skipping breakfast and having Domino's for lunch?

Some of you may argue that it's actually more expensive to eat healthily, and you know what, I agree. Sadly, the way our economy is set up here in the UK is to encourage us to not look after ourselves, to eat fast food and watch TV. The price of a McDonalds is far less than buying food from a shop and meal prepping it the night before. But we're all playing the game of life, and that game is a marathon, not a sprint (although life does go pretty fast). We enjoy the benefits of investing in our health early on in life by preventing disease and illness later. The price of a chicken salad or meal-prepped salmon and vegetables doesn't sound so bad when you compare it to weeks of private healthcare for digestive issues later on in life.

Aside from the prevention of health issues, there are plenty of other positives that eating a healthy lunch will expose us to, like releasing endorphins to help with stress on a busy day, strengthening our bones and muscles to get those big recruitment arms or washboard abs we all so stereotypically desire, and improving brain health and cognitive function.

There may be some people reading this who didn't have the luxury of being exposed to healthy eating and fitness habits while growing up. You may be genuinely unsure on what to eat and when to eat it. I'd encourage you to speak to someone who can help – a personal trainer, nutritionist or even a friend who's really into the gym. As someone who's been into fitness my whole life, with a well-rounded, healthy diet (most of the time), I'll happily summarise what is generally wise to eat at lunchtime to maximise productivity. There are some fundamental basics that we should stick to, especially on the days we're sitting down for the majority of our time. We want to avoid any fast or processed food. Period. Our body finds these hard to digest, and it requires more energy to do so, which is often why you get that sluggish feeling after eating some fast food. We probably want to give high carbohydrate meals a miss for lunch, too. Something like a pasta dish might leave us feeling stodgy and unmotivated to get through the afternoon. Instead, we should prioritise a high protein meal, with some healthy fats and a small amount of carbs.

The possibilities of what we can eat are endless, but it's

always a good idea to meal prep something for the week. It saves money compared to eating out on the daily, and you know exactly what's in your meal. A solid bit of advice I was given many years ago is that we should be able to know exactly how we will feel after a meal. Eating something light, healthy and protein-dense will provide you with a second wind in the afternoon to speak to those prospects or candidates. If you can flip your mindset when it comes to eating for energy and productivity, rather than taste and comfort, at least in the week, you'll see your output and mood change for the better.

Tip Six
Everyone Wants a Hollywood Star

*'If you don't produce, you won't thrive –
no matter how skilled or talented you are.'*
Cal Newport, American author and professor

Hollywood, a place renowned for its ability to attract the global powerhouses that are actors, musicians, sport stars and celebrities. Everyone wants to know someone in Hollywood, and I imagine most people would love the opportunity to employ someone who's in Hollywood, too. For context, I'm referring to a Hollywood star as a candidate who possesses all or nearly all the relevant skills for a job. Finding a Hollywood star for your client is often unlikely, and there usually needs to be some flexibility in certain areas, but every now and then you'll find someone that will blow everyone out of the water. It's a great feeling.

But to find that superstar for your client, you have to be in it to win it. How can we expect to find that ideal person if we don't start with a 'Hollywood Search'? What is a Hollywood

Search? Well, to explain, let's first start with something more familiar.

In this modern world of recruitment, I find it hard to believe that anyone makes regular placements without use of the Boolean search. Would you believe that the Boolean search was invented all the way back in 1847 by an English mathematician and philosopher, George Boole. Although it started out as an algebraic system of logic, the concept has been adjusted and developed and since been used in a variety of ways. Us recruiters aren't known for being the sharpest tools in the shed, so it took some time for our industry to adopt it. Even as recently thirty years ago, a recruiter asked to run a Boolean search would have looked like they'd just been asked to peel an orange with no hands. It's not until the last twenty years that the Boolean search gained an increase in usage in recruitment. (Although there may be a few veterans of the game reading this who've been using it since 1980s; I see you, Clive.)

These days, if you ask any recruiter, whether that's permanent, contract, agency or in-house, a Boolean search is probably their most effective way of finding candidates. Most of us will use a Boolean search on a daily basis, sometimes up to fifteen or twenty times a day depending on variations and job flow. The Hollywood Search is a way of employing a Boolean search to shoot for the stars: to try and find the one perfect candidate.

I've done well not to mention AI until tip six, but in the not-too-distant future we will likely see a day when an AI tool can create complex Booleans for us. For now, alongside some already decent Boolean builders out there, SourceBreaker as an example, it's best we master the art of a well architected search ourselves, allowing us to search different engines and websites more deeply.

In basic terms, a Hollywood Search is when we utilise a Boolean search that includes every single key criterion required for that candidate to be considered a perfect match. Or as I like to phrase it, a Hollywood star. To effectively run a Hollywood Search, we need to have invested time and effort into truly understanding the job brief from the client. You should have discussed what is non-negotiable, and what the client may be able to flex on. If you have asked the right questions, you will know what is required to set a great candidate apart from an excellent one.

Let's say you want a dog – not just any dog though, you'd like an Italian Greyhound. You'd like it to be a blue colour, no older than six months, local to Bristol, to have all its jabs and be a male. You might be willing to consider a dog that's older than six months, and you might consider a black one, but it absolutely *has* to be male, have its jabs and be local to Bristol.

Now we've established all this information, we can start our Hollywood Search and then work backwards in order of importance. A search of 'Italian Greyhound' and 'blue' and 'jabs' and 'bristol' and 'under six months' may only allow us a small market of, let's say, two dogs. However, these would be exactly the right dogs, dogs with the potential to be your Hollywood star.

That being said, two people is a small pond to fish from. What happens if they're not in the market, have just changed roles or are out of your salary range? That brings us to our process of working backwards by order of importance. To go back to my example, we could run the search again, taking away the colour 'blue' but keeping all of our other criteria, exposing us to a bigger market of, let's say, eighteen dogs. This now allows us a healthy talent, or dog-ownership, pool of candidates to approach. Alternatively, you could play around with your searches and customise as necessary. Let's imagine adding 'blue' back in but removing 'under six months'. Or adding 'black' rather than 'blue'. There will be multiple variations for you to create until you get back to the bare minimum your client will consider a viable candidate to invite for an interview.

Generally, your first Hollywood Search will have a small number of profiles or candidates to approach. As you work back, dropping one criterion at a time, the available candidates should increase. If your searches aren't providing many candidates even after you've scaled back your Hollywood Search, it might be wise to have that conversation with your client to manage expectations. From the client's perspective, after briefing you on all their nice-to-haves and would-ideally-likes, there will be nothing worse than for you to come back with the minimum standards. An Italian greyhound with its jabs, but white and located in Portsmouth – would you, or your client, be happy with that? Communication and assuring your client on what's realistic is a vital part of managing any process effectively.

Tip Seven
Turn Up Fifteen Minutes Early Everywhere You Go

'Either you run the day or the day runs you.'
Jim Rohn, American entrepreneur and author

There are lots of resources in this world: natural, capital, economic… Yet there is only one that is truly finite, and that's time. Time is the only resource in the world that we can't get back. We can, however, choose to invest our time wisely.

Without getting too philosophical, we have a limited time on this earth, eighty years if we're lucky, and then we die. We're all getting out the same way, so effectively managing our time is a skill that is utterly indispensable for living a fulfilled life and achieving success. It takes a good amount of self-discipline to manage and respect our time effectively, but it can be made easier when we look at time as a resource that we must invest in order to achieve what we want.

Turn Up Fifteen Minutes Early Everywhere You Go | 33

Now I've got you thinking about your limited time on earth, and just how important it is to spend our time wisely, how do you think other people feel when we don't respect their time? Someone has decided that seeing you is worth an hour that they can never be refunded. I think it's only fair that we treat that with the utmost appreciation.

Like most skills shared in this book, and in life in general, good timekeeping is a habit. All habits need conscious awareness and to be consistently repeated to become a core part of our routine. When I meet someone who respects both their own and other people's time, I instantly have admiration for them, because it doesn't come easy. It's a true sign of self-discipline and organisation.

It may sound extreme, but if you asked anyone close to me, they'd tell you that I would be early for my own execution day. There's not a single event, activity or appointment that I wouldn't be fifteen minutes early for. It's an ongoing joke with my friends and colleagues that if we're ever meeting somewhere, they know the chances are I'll be the first there. In the sagacious words of William Shakespeare, 'Better three hours too soon than a minute too late'. This attitude has served me well in recruitment.

What areas of your professional career can you analyse to see if you're really valuing your own time? Let's start with our daily routine, the structure of our day. Things might have been slightly different for most of us over the last few years with remote working, but the tides have turned and the recruitment industry is back to being predominantly on site, which means our days usually start with some sort of travel to an office. For me, at least in the early years of your recruitment career, you *must* be getting in at least fifteen minutes before your clock in time. There's a big long list of reasons why, but I'll share the top few, the ones that have kept me turning up early day after day.

Firstly, we want to be setting the standard: setting the standard not only for ourselves, but also for our colleagues and our competition. It's no secret that there's an air of respect around the office for someone who gets in early; it represents hunger, ambition, drive and purpose. I've worked in various places over my career, and the person first in, or at least earlier than most, is usually the person creating their own luck and billing the most.

Another reason is to sit down, gather your thoughts and plan your day without getting caught in the morning 'How was your weekend?' chat. This conversation can drag on throughout the day and into the early parts of Tuesday. Each to their own; for some this might contribute to their happiness and wellbeing at work, and I encourage that. But I'm writing from the perspective of becoming the best. What if your competition is turning up forty-five minutes before you clock in, and they've already spoken to the three best candidates new to the market before you've even checked your emails?

Throughout the rest of our day and week, we will most likely have multiple time blocks, various internal meetings and new business appointments. These will most likely consist of calls and hopefully meetings with candidates, prospects and existing customers, all of which deserve thoughtfulness. When it's time to plan your route to these meetings, make it requisite that your arrival time be a minimum of fifteen minutes before time. How many times in your life have you left for something important, and you've allowed yourself a measly five minutes to spare? The world works in a strange way sometimes, and it's

Turn Up Fifteen Minutes Early Everywhere You Go | 35

no coincidence that if you fail to prepare, you prepare to fail. You might encounter traffic, unexpected roadworks, or leave something you need at home, and suddenly you're on the brink of ruining your day. But with fifteen minutes' leeway, barring major disaster, you will still arrive on time; in the best case scenario, you're fifteen minutes early, relaxed and have created the impression that you're someone who respects people's time. And don't forget to let the other party know you have arrived early. It creates a good impression.

I hope you can use common sense when choosing to abide by the golden fifteen minutes role. I don't need to tell you that it would be a complete waste of time to turn up so early to an internal meeting, right? Walking to a meeting room which is fifteen feet away, to sit there in anticipation, is no way to demonstrate how efficient you are.

Being early is a way of life, and once you commit to it, you can't go back. Even the potential of being a few minutes late, even simply only on time, will send you into a rage, and rightly so. Other people's time should be treated as royalty, and if you want to build a reputation for yourself as someone who's respectful, efficient and courteous, this is the place to start.

Tip Eight
Dress for the Day You Want to Have

'You can have anything you want in life if you dress for it.'
Edith Head, American costume designer

Humans are judgemental creatures by nature. Our subconscious mind analyses people and things and makes assumptions based on past experiences or events. Whether we like it or not, most of us judge other people by their physical appearance – their clothes, hair, smell, shoes, bag or even their walk. When we see a man walking down the street in a three-piece suit with his hair done and smelling of Tom Ford, if you're like me, you'll be curious as to where he's going or what he does. Or a lady who's in a flattering dress, heels, a nice bag, has her hair blow dried and oozes Baccarat Rouge – it's more than likely we'll turn our head and ponder on who she is or where she's going.

Dressing appropriately for the day you want isn't just important for your appearance to others. Yes, a smart, well-dressed individual will create a strong impression, increasing their chances of meeting the right people, but more importantly, dressing well sets the tone for ourselves. By making a conscious effort with our appearance, wearing clothes that make us look and feel good, we're telling ourselves we're ready and we deserve the opportunities coming our way. I genuinely believe we create our own luck in life, and this is one area you can stand out from the crowd.

Have you ever seen a successful CEO turn up to an important day, or any day for that matter, in tracksuit bottoms? Or how about an ambitious managing director turning up to their office wearing gym wear, knowing she has scheduled meetings that day? It's highly unlikely in the world of recruitment. Ben Francis, the founder of Gymshark, may turn up in gym wear, but that's *his* branded gym wear. And anyway, he operates in that industry, not recruitment. I know and have met plenty of top performers in recruitment and sales throughout my years, and almost all of them take pride in their appearance.

I'm grateful that the modernised world of recruitment is a bit more fluid than it used to be. Most industries and companies have moved away from suits and heels every day, and there are a few reasons why I believe that's of benefit. Luckily for most in recruitment, we are fortunate to be treated like adults, often given core hours and flexibility to be where we need to be, as well as being given free rein to dress however we feel necessary. It is still smart casual for most, but some have adopted the policy of *anything* goes. There are recruiters that turn up to work in gym wear, a tracksuit, or who just have little regard for how much their appearance contributes to their success. If this is you, this is not a personal attack, but rather an option to consider a different perspective, one that you may not have considered before.

You're a recruiter, and whether we want to accept it or not, recruitment is a sales role. Lead generation and hunting down new business is one of our biggest responsibilities. Above all, this requires the right mindset and attitude, and I can assure you that yours will change depending on the way you've put yourself together that day: the clothes you've decided for that day, how you've positioned your hair, and so on. These decisions are statements we make about ourselves; they're no different to affirmations we might say to the mirror.

I hope that all of you reading this have been lucky enough to have had the opportunity to dress up to the max once or twice. If you haven't, you should most definitely try to find an occasion. For those of you who have had such a chance, I want you to mentally visualise those times. What were you wearing? How much effort did you put into your appearance? How did you feel that day? Did you receive any compliments? How were you treated? What did that do for your confidence? What luck might have come your way? A wedding or an awards ceremony are prime examples of when we may get the chance to put some effort in, and I would bet most of us feel good on these occasions. One compliment can change the trajectory of your whole mood for the day. A conversation sparked simply by your looking like someone of importance could completely alter the rest of your year.

Do we really need to wait for a special occasion to take our attitude into our own hands? To create a stronger perception of ourselves in the world? We all have more days that feel mundane and repetitive than days when we get the opportunity to dress up and enjoy ourselves. Doesn't that make you think? You might not be bothered to make an effort for twenty-nine days of the month, because it's just a typical rainy week in the middle of March. And it *is* an effort to iron your clothes the night before, or to get up thirty minutes earlier to do your hair. But effort is what it takes to hit your goals and chase your dreams.

I think some of us are genuinely scared of what would happen if we decided to dress for the day we want every day. How would our colleagues and friends start treating us differently? What opportunities might just present themselves to us? Who might we get to rub shoulders with just because of the way we've put ourselves together?

I'd like to close out this tip by acknowledging that dressing well and smelling good can appear a huge financial cost. But consider it an investment into your career progression. To take pride in yourself, you don't need high-end or designer clothes. Rather clothes that fit you well, colours that complement your skin or eyes, and an aftershave or perfume that lets people know you look after yourself. Once you start consciously getting dressed in the morning, with the attitude of attacking that day, you'll see your results will change considerably and your influence on others increase.

Tip Nine
Master Your Pre-Meeting Rituals

'Lost time is never found again.'
Benjamin Franklin, polymath and founding father
of the United States

When the time comes to meet a prospective client, it's usually after many weeks of consistent work. Knowing the effort we've put in to get some quality time in front of our prospect, doesn't it make sense to increase our attention to detail and leave nothing to chance? Aside from making a placement, meeting with a prospect is one of the most exciting times in recruitment. It's an opportunity to make a good first impression, the start of building a new professional relationship and, hopefully, securing some new business. Sadly, in this crazy recruitment world there is a phenomenon where prospects will flirtatiously give you all the buying signals you need, even going so far as to book the meeting, only to not show up on the day. If it has happened to you, don't worry, you're not alone, and if it hasn't yet, buckle up: it will and it's not something you ever get used to.

Master Your Pre-Meeting Rituals | 41

What we need to understand is that the time between when your prospect says yes to the meeting, and the day of the actual meeting itself, is an important valley of death that requires tactical updates and communication. As we know, prospects are busy, so meetings often get booked a week in advance, in busier periods sometimes two or even three weeks into the future. From experience, and as you would have probably guessed, it's always best to book meetings to take place as soon as possible, to keep momentum.

Think about it from your perspective: you've booked a meeting with a potential new client three weeks in advance, but you don't hear from them once in that three weeks, not even on the day; anyone in their right mind is going to consider cancelling. As a rule of thumb, we should be following up with an email every week until the meeting's due date. Think about how much can change in our world in a single week; it's likely to be the same in a prospect's week, maybe even more so. It's worth mentioning that the weekly email follow-ups must add value. There is no quicker way to disengage a potential client's interest than repeatedly asking if they're 'still ok' for the meeting every week during the build-up. Instead, add value: tell them about some changes in the market, share with them some recent company news or ask them questions about their world.

When we email to reinstate the meeting on the day, we're not simply asking if they're still OK to attend, far from it: we're looking to add as much value as possible. This is the perfect opportunity for a confirmation about the specific problems you spoke about previously, or some changes in the service/market that you plan to discuss.

You might not get a response to this email, and that's OK;

our main objective remains reconfirming the reason for the meetings, and that we still intend to attend. I can guarantee they will read the email if they have some time booked in the diary with you. This meeting will be as important to them as it is to us. After all, we are offering a solution to a problem they're currently facing.

When the big day has come around, providing the meeting has been correctly qualified and regular communication consistent, it's showtime. One of the best feelings in recruitment is the excitement of possibly bringing on a new logo to do business with. Whether or not you've taken on board the previous chapter, a new business meeting is the day you *definitely* put on your best outfit, do your hair (if you have any left; it is recruitment after all), do your makeup if you wear any, and make yourself smell nice.

I've been using the tactic of confirming on the day for many years, and for me it's a non-negotiable. Some may tell you to confirm the day before, which is ok, but a lot can change overnight, and emergencies do happen. There's a multitude of reasons why we confirm on the day, but they can all be encapsulated by one term: making a solid first impression. We want to confirm our meetings as soon as we physically can, and for me that is usually at 5am, just after I wake. You may think that 5am is too early, but what counts is the impact it has on the prospect once they see that email (email, don't text that early on). Plus, I'm up at that time, so why not? Fortunately for any of you who like to sleep in a little later, we now live in an age where we can schedule emails and texts.

When someone gets up and checks their emails and we're the first person to email that day, sharing our excitement and our commitment to that meeting, what image of ourselves are

Master Your Pre-Meeting Rituals | 43

we creating for that prospect? Someone who's efficient, organised, excited, passionate and professional. Also, sending an email that early almost always breaks the ice when you finally meet. It usually provokes a reaction that is a combination of shock and impressed, and it will always get you off to a good start.

So that we're all on the same page, our confirmation email should assume that the meeting is still going ahead. 'Are you still on for today?' should never be used, no matter how doubtful you are that the meeting will take place. Providing someone with an option will almost certainly prompt a cancellation. Typically, it's good to share that you're looking forward to the meeting for x reason and that you plan to cover y problem.

Let's be realistic, you can go through all this work and a small number may still cancel or rearrange. But the finer details that can be incorporated into our process reduces the risk. If you're someone who has a high cancellation or no-show rate, it may be time to look at why this might be. There will be an abundance of reasons, some out of your control, but a lack of communication or reassurances along the way could well be one of them.

Tip Ten
Prioritise Lead Generation Every Day

'You are out of business if you don't have a prospect.'
Zig Ziglar, American author and motivational speaker

In the words of Gary Kelleher in his book *The One Thing*, 'Not everything matters equally, and success isn't a game won by whoever does the most. Yet that is exactly how most play it on a daily basis. Until my ONE Thing is done—everything else is a distraction.'

To apply this to the world of recruitment, I'd debate anyone that lead generation is our ONE thing: everything else, relatively speaking, is a distraction. The process of identifying and cultivating potential customers for our businesses and markets is sacrosanct, and we should be scheduling time to do this every day, and during the periods we feel most productive. Scheduling our day with planned times to find these leads is a sure way to become an overachiever.

On the topic of scheduling times for important tasks, I read a book called *Eat That Frog* by Brian Tracy, which explains to

Prioritise Lead Generation Every Day | 45

the reader that, if you had to eat a frog every day, it would be better to eat that frog as early as possible, to just get it done so you could go about your day. Eating a frog first thing would be unpleasant to say the least, and it's no surprise that in business the most important tasks we need to complete are often also the unpleasant, least enjoyable tasks, like making sales calls and prioritising leads.

But to really flourish in our recruitment careers, successfully managing our pipeline is absolutely compulsory. The good news is we can take complete ownership of our pipeline by doing just one thing: consistently generating leads. That's the good news, but depending on how you feel about lead generation, there's some not so good news too: the work never stops. There will *never* be a time where we aren't developing new leads, fishing for information and finding new clients to work with. If the thought of generating leads every day for the rest of your career hasn't scared you off, and you're able to progressively build your pipeline with leads daily, weekly and monthly, you can be assured that you'll be in the top end of recruitment professionals. Anyone who can accurately forecast how likely they are to achieve their targets month by month is guaranteed to outperform someone who isn't able to do so.

Before you read on, I would like you to think, maybe even write down, five different ways you can generate leads in a typical day of recruitment. Got five? Let's see what you've got. My list includes the following: asking candidates where they are interviewing on calls, looking on job boards to see which companies are actively hiring, cold calling prospects to hear about their hiring plans, attending networking events, asking current clients for referrals, taking references from candidates you're working with to speak to new hiring managers for any potential replacements, targeted social marketing campaigns (paid or free), free content such as blogs or articles, personalised email marketing and discounts or offers. That's ten, and I'm sure, with the ever-improving world of marketing, there may be some more. Incorporating even half of these into our daily habits and routines will undoubtedly improve our ability to pull in leads and build a solid pipeline. Can you imagine the amount of leads you would have if you asked every single candidate you speak to where they are interviewing? Or you made forty sales calls per week rather than twenty? How about asking every client that you've invoiced this year for one referral to a company that's recruiting? It's phenomenal how much us recruiters leave on the table sometimes.

For anyone that has already built good habits around lead generation, you'll be no stranger to the fact that there are often times when someone won't tell you where they are interviewing, or a client won't know anyone to refer to you. But I'm sure all of us would have at some point heard 'If you don't ask you don't get.' As recruiters, we need to feel comfortable asking for more. Top billers and overachievers who've been in the industry for years will understand the importance of hot leads and a blooming pipeline, and probably won't need to convince themselves to schedule time nor remind themselves to do so. It's a natural instinct for anyone who's on the top of their game. When self-esteem is high and you're on an upwards trajectory, it's only right you have the confidence to ask these sorts of questions. 'A company is recruiting and they aren't using me? Ludicrous! I'm not having that!' I'm sure that will resonate with some of you; I know it does with me at times.

Prioritise Lead Generation Every Day | 47

For those who are still in the process of making a mark and building their brand, it's best to schedule time in your diary specifically for lead generation. For me, the two most efficient ways to generate leads in an external role are speaking to candidates on the phone, and cold calling prospective new clients. These two tasks receive a minimum of one hour per day every single day. Referencing Brian Tracy and the analogy of eating the frog first thing, I've often found I have more energy and mental capacity in the morning, so that's the time I'll make my sales calls, usually for an hour (or two) between 8am and 11am. Depending on my success, I often find it beneficial to complete a second power hour just after lunch.

Likewise, I schedule a time to actively speak to candidates with the sole purpose of generating leads. For me, this would typically be between 11-12 and 4-5. The times aren't actually that important, and depending on the industry you're in they may vary, but you should be able to calculate when you're most likely to get hold of candidates. Outside of regular meeting times, over lunch periods and later into the evening are three of the most common. For anyone who is new to recruitment, I'll let you into a little secret: there will be times when you'll be oversubscribed with the amount of jobs you'll be working, but this is indubitably when you most need to generate leads. There have been many occasions in my own career, and I've also seen it in others', where us recruiters we will be comfortable with the amount of jobs we have, believing our own hype and thinking this place of luxury will last forever. The word complacency springs to mind, and complacent recruiters don't make it to the top of their industry. Prioritise lead generation every day, and watch your pipeline grow and your results multiply.

Tip Eleven
No Update Is Still an Update

'In teamwork, silence isn't golden, it's deadly'
Mark Sanborn, American entrepreneur, author
and professional speaker

If I can ask you to promise me that you'll take at least one tip away from this book, this is the one. I encourage you to read it more than once, and to ponder it for as long as you need. This might be one of the most important tips for anyone in recruitment, whether it's your first day or you're twenty years deep.

Recruitment professionals can regularly be on the receiving end of derogatory comments. I'm a recruitment business owner who takes my career extraordinarily seriously and would debate anyone who says we are paid too well or disregards our contributions to most industries. But I can admit there are a handful of things we as an industry can do better. Some of these aren't just applicable to the world of recruitment: they are human traits, such as lack of communication, which can be found in almost every industry. But us recruiters take the brunt of the slander.

The art of communication is a dying skill in recruitment, and arguably the world as we know it. With the modern world changing literally every day, everyone's focus is on AI and how it can improve our lives. To not stray off on a tangent about AI – because I could be there for a while – I'd like us all to be aware of how important human communication remains in an industry where our 'product' is a human being. As Oprah Winfrey says, 'Great communication starts with connection', and with a connection comes the chance to build a relationship, increase engagement, and the ability to avoid any misunderstandings. If us recruiters understood that 90% of our role is effectively communicating, we would without a doubt make sure we became effective communicators.

One of the main reasons the recruitment industry takes a bashing is because of ghosting. Ghosting, for anyone not familiar with the term, is when someone suddenly withdraws from communication without letting the other person know, often never to be heard from again. Again, ghosting is common in almost any profession you can think of, but because the recruitment process isn't *particularly* enjoyable for the job seeker, any lapse in communication is often met with particular repugnance. To be fair, some candidates put all their trust in us to find for them the next step in their career, so I can understand the frustration. What I won't ever understand is why there is so often an urge to slate the industry as a whole, neglecting all previous positive experiences with recruiters because of being ghosted once or twice.

Rationally I believe there are two reasons why a recruiter might be a regular offender when it comes to ghosting.

33 Ways to Become a Better Recruiter (and Human)

Firstly, and I'll say this bluntly, it could be because you just don't care deeply enough. You might not yet sufficiently value the individual you're supporting, and your reputation in the market. And if you don't value these two, you almost certainly won't care about the negative perception of yourself that you're allowing to blossom. At the core of recruitment are selfless activities: helping individuals find their dream roles and serving clients to fulfil orders and scale their teams. But this is too easily forgotten in our busy periods, when we're doing well, or even when we may be struggling. When we recognize that being altruistic benefits us in the longer term, we'll change the narrative of our industry.

Secondly, and most importantly, us recruiters seem to forget that the candidates we support are actual human beings. Throughout our days and working weeks, the thrills of recruitment are likely to serve us a wave of emotions ranging from overwhelming excitement and joy to cataclysmic disappointment and apprehension about the future. What makes us think that the humans we serve don't experience similar feelings? They will unquestionably be met with excitement when we share new opportunities with them, they will no doubt face anxious thoughts when they don't hear from us and are waiting for feedback, and I can guarantee they will almost always need extra support with their interview preparation. Recruitment is a team sport.

A mantra I adopted way back in my early days was that I would treat every candidate as if they were my immediate family. By immediate family, I mean my mum, dad, sister or even a cousin. Remembering this when I'm introduced to a new candidate has improved my communication exponentially. Think about it, how would you treat your brother or

No Update Is Still an Update | 51

sister if you were supporting them in finding their next career move? I find it hard to believe that anyone reading this wouldn't go above and beyond. You would try to find them the best opportunities and provide them with regular updates. There's no denying you would make sure they were over-prepared for every interview and sent into the interview with your encouragement and best wishes.

The overarching purpose of this tip is to encourage you to communicate more, and the 'no update is still an update' principle reminds us to do so even when things are progressing slowly. It doesn't matter if you're in-house, agency or even a stakeholder who partakes in recruitment occasionally. If we're representing candidates in an application process, ideally we should be updating them by phone or text every twenty-four hours, even if there's no update. Depending on how urgent the vacancy of a client is, we might also want to update them via email every twenty-four hours too, regardless of the progression we've made. Being an in-house recruiter also comes with its challenges, and regular communication and updates with internal stakeholders are vital to build a strong bond.

It doesn't need to be a call every time, but perhaps a simple LinkedIn message, text or email, which takes no more than thirty seconds. Candidates appreciate this more than you will ever know. I've had candidates turn around and tell me thanks, but they don't need this many updates and just to let them know when I get feedback. I've also had candidates express their gratitude to me for keeping them updated when times are tough. Different responses, and we may want to adjust our approach accordingly, but notice what they have in common? They both express gratitude.

We absolutely do not want to be in a position where the candidate has had to chase us up more than once. That's the biggest sign that we aren't communicating enough and providing regular updates. Recruitment is a revolving door: hiring managers will most likely become candidates, and candidates will undoubtedly become hiring managers, so treat everyone with equal respect and provide updates. As Maya Angelou once said, 'I've learned that people will forget what you said, people will forget what you did, but people will never forget how you made them feel.'

Tip Twelve
Invest in a Diary and Plan Your Days

'An hour of planning can save you ten hours of doing.'
Dale Carnegie, American writer and lecturer

Aside from Dale Carnegie's words of wisdom above, there is only one quote more profound and relevant to the significance of planning in recruitment, and it's courtesy of the great Benjamin Franklin: 'By failing to prepare, you are preparing to fail.' To allow ourselves the best chances of an affluent career in recruitment, planning our days and planning ahead is simply indispensable. With well-planned days come well-planned weeks then well-planned months, and that level of attention to the detail is required to be an adept recruiter.

As humans, we are hardwired to gravitate towards certain things. These drives are amplified in some people, me being one of them, and not so apparent in others, but I'd like to think most people in recruitment fall into the former category. They're things like routine, the drive to create structure and stability in our life, our natural desire to be productive and work through a task list. But most powerful of all, we humans strive for a sense of achievement; we desire to be on the path to success.

Planning our days is one of the only tasks we can do on a daily basis that will allow us to achieve these drives. When I talk about planning a day effectively, it's a mix of time blocks for our most important tasks, reminders of internal and external meetings, sufficient time to prepare for these, and then the time to attend to those smaller tasks which won't make the top of our list but are still of importance, like following up with a specific candidate about a certain role. Having this information displayed clearly in a diary will allow you to feel like you have real control of the day. As well as controlling the day, working through and checking off our tasks releases dopamine in short bursts. Our brain's feel-good chemical, dopamine is why, as humans, we enjoy getting things done. We feel a real sense of achievement if we manage to work through all our important tasks for the day, and that's critical to looking after our mental health.

There's no denying we're living in the 'future', and our technology-driven world is escalating at a pace like never before. There's a new app available to us almost every week, a new service that promises to revolutionise the way we do things. There are probably hundreds of apps, alongside built-in calendars on email platforms like Gmail and Outlook, that allow us to plan and schedule an online diary. Online diaries are good, and there's a time and a place for them; they're quick and easy, and they provide useful notifications. That being said, I'm a fan of science-backed evidence, and there are many physiological and neuroscientific publications online that share the benefits of writing things down. Writing things down

Invest in a Diary and Plan Your Days | 55

not only makes us more effective, it gives us a greater chance of accomplishing a goal – according to a study by author Mark Fisher in a publication on leadership called *Are Smart Goals Dumb?*, almost 1.4 times greater. Writing out our tasks and day plans improves our overall productivity, whilst unburdening our working memory. Our brains are incredible machines, but it's no secret that we have a limited capacity to remember things, and offloading tasks by writing them down can free up space for more important information. All of this takes that extra bit of effort, but if we show a stronger commitment to a task or a goal if it is written down and in front of us, surely that's worth the effort?

Ask yourself how often you write out your day plans. How about your weekly plans? I'd almost guarantee that most of us could be doing more, including me. Where I'm at now in my recruitment career, I try to write down my day plans the night before, and my weekly plans on a Sunday. I have a list of tasks that are categorised by level of importance, and I'll make sure those are worked through the following day. Recruitment can be disorderly and confusing some days, and this is intensified without a clear plan of attack for the day ahead.

This is why a physical diary is indispensable to overachieving in your recruitment career. There have been periods of time where I have been in-between diaries, or out of love with my daily writing, and I noticed a clear difference in my structure, mental focus and ability to perform. If I have inspired you enough to invest in a new diary, there has never been a better time to do so. We live in a time when productivity diaries, or daily planners, are now produced by a number of different companies and the quality is increasing year on year. You can pick up some incredible diaries online, so don't settle for an

A4 pad because you're on a budget. A diary is an investment into your future success. Every one of us will look for different qualities, but in an ideal world you'll want a diary that allows a detailed daily plan, a less focused weekly plan and bird's-eye view monthly plans. Some extra nice-to-haves could be a daily habit tracker, a full-day eating schedule, an option to write out your own daily quote (my favourite of them all), or maybe a daily gratitude section.

If you want to be unstoppable, you need to slow down to speed up. Take the time to plan your days effectively by writing them down to help boost your connection to your goals. I have no affiliations with any brands, but I'm a generous person, so I'd encourage you to look at Papier or Mal Paper, who have the best diaries in my opinion.

Tip Thirteen
Get Face Time with Your Clients

*'If you believe a business is built on relationships,
make building them your business.'*
Scott Stratten, American author

The world as we know it has changed. When I first started writing this book, I planned to avoid the word 'Covid-19', but there's no getting around it: it's played a huge part in shaping the future of the recruitment industry. Throughout the challenging times of this pandemic, the recruitment industry was shaken to its core. With that came some positive changes, changes that are here to stay, and some not so positive changes that I think we could consider a different approach to.

We're now cemented in a digital world, but I'd like you to think back to pre-2020 and how we typically conducted business. Despite what some people may think, online calls using the likes of Zoom and Teams weren't that popular before 2020, at least not in my world. If we ever had a new business meeting, our default approach was to organise something either at their offices, our offices or a mutual location. All new business opportunities and existing business reviews were conducted in person, simple as that. As long as the length of the journey was worth the return on investment, day trips on the train to London were normal and driving up to an hour or so was treated as standard.

One positive that I believe came from the unprecedented times of the early 2020s was how quickly the world decided that we could all work remotely. For most companies, this was a first, and not many knew what they were doing, how they would still achieve results let alone actually thrive. Then Zoom came along; you could call it an overnight success, but like most of these, it actually took nine years to get there. CNN reports that on March 23rd, 2020, Zoom was downloaded a mind-boggling 2.13 million times, up from 2.04 million times the day before. Two months prior, the app had just under 56,000 global downloads in a day. The rise of Zoom allowed us to connect digitally with friends, colleagues, clients and even potential new business. To say it revolutionised the way most businesses operate would be an understatement.

We are more digitally connected than ever before, but when we take time to think about it, I'd argue we're the least connected we have ever been. It's no secret we are still becoming accustomed to the digital world, and I think that's because of the speed of the advancements we experience every day.

The mass introduction of online calls and remote working has benefited recruitment in a number of ways. Companies, particularly in tech, have been able to recruit, hire and onboard new employees globally. I've worked with engineers

Get Face Time with Your Clients | 59

based in the UK who have been lucky enough to work for companies out in Silicon Valley or New York. Companies that have adopted this approach have access to the best talent in the market. However, as restrictions eased and we welcomed back some 'normality', for the most part companies opted for hybrid working, some even full time on-site. What the recruitment industry *did* do was move completely to online calls, and that has clawed back one of our most valuable assets back: time.

To start with internal communications, online calls allow meetings across multiple different office locations. On top of this, recruiters can now develop and win business outside of their geographical locations. Let's not misconstrue what I am trying to get across here, I know a lot of UK-based companies have been operating UK-wide, even in Europe and the USA, for a long time; but 2020 was when the rest of the recruitment industry caught up. What used to be a three-hour roundtrip for the opportunity of speaking to a new potential client can now be organised online. This not only saves time, but finances, so it's no wonder it's become the most popular way of communication, and there's no denying that it's here to stay.

But here's the thing, humans thrive on human interaction. Dating back as far as we know, we've built relationships, sold services and socialised in person, face to face; only in the last decade or two has that switched to the digital world. We are intelligent creatures and have in-built systems that can consciously and subconsciously pick up on an array of nonverbal cues, like facial expressions, eye movements and body language. All of this is equally, if not more important than the words that come out of our mouths. There's something powerful about sitting opposite another individual, whether a friend, a prospect or an existing customer, looking into the whites of their eyes and talking business. Face-to-face meetings allow us to strengthen our connections to our clients, and with most other recruiters deciding to sit behind the screen, you put yourself at a huge advantage by getting out in front of them.

If geography allows, meeting a client or prospective client to shake their hand and welcome them with a warm smile should be prioritised over an online call. The difference in the levels of excitement when you have a meeting booked in person compared to something online is extraordinary. Waking up with a new business meeting in the diary creates a buzz. It's time to dress slightly better than usual, put some wet look gel in your hair, or makeup on your face, and be ready to attack that day. Even in 2024, you and your colleagues should be prioritising face-to-face time with clients.

I'm not against online calls. I utilise them most weeks. But if you have paying clients who regularly give you opportunities and support your business, these are the clients you need to prioritise with your presence. And not just with meetings, but coffees, dinners and events. To stand out from the crowd, ask to meet people; I can assure you that most of the industry will default to an online call.

Tip Fourteen
Study Your Competition

*'The supreme art of war is to subdue
the enemy without fighting.'*
Sun Tzu, Chinese general and strategist

Recruitment is a fiercely competitive industry, with everyone contesting to be a top biller or at least a person of influence in their market. Whether you're building a market in tech, construction or finance, in the UK, US or Europe, you're almost guaranteed to encounter a good amount of competition who are looking to take some of your market share. So if competition is inevitable, what do we do about it?

Fortunately for us, the study of knowing our competition, what they do, how they operate, their strengths and their weaknesses, has been at the forefront of the minds of some history's greatest leaders, dating as far back as 544 BC. The earliest and most prolific figure when it comes to studying the competition is Sun Tzu, but some other influential names you may recognise could be John D. Rockefeller, Franklin D. Roosevelt and

Genghis Khan. All four of these men had something in common: they were all at the top of their game, with men competing to take their spot, even their lives in some cases. These four men understood the importance of not only knowing their competition inside and out but having a strategy to destroy them, by any means.

You might think fighting in a war is a *little bit* different to working in recruitment, and you'd be quite right. But whether we're building a business, competing in any sort of sporting event, or trying to earn a promotion at work, the same principles apply. Choosing not to understand our competition puts us at a huge disadvantage to those who do.

For example, if you're working in a software engineering niche in the UK, focusing on a specific coding language and a certain geographical location, chances are there're twenty maybe even thirty people also operating in that niche. Finding out every single person who you're competing against should be your number one priority. Where are they based? What companies do they work with? What do they do well? What do you do better than them? We're not on about stalking someone here, before I get you into trouble, but they need to be on your radar. Are they attending more networking events than you? Do they start work an hour before you every single day? Are they currently on maternity leave and can you approach their clients? What we need to acknowledge is their genuine ability to perform their job, their character and what special traits they possess, when they might be at a certain location, or specific event, what clients they seem to be regularly working with, and why these candidates enjoy working with them more than anyone else.

Do you think Sun Tzu, a Chinese military general and strategist,

Study Your Competition | 63

would have been so successful if he didn't study his competition? In his book *The Art of War*, Sun Tzu explains how so much of his success was down to understanding his enemies. The best result, he wrote, was 'to subdue the enemy without fighting' and to do so one had to understand 'what is strong, and strike at what is weak'.

And let's face it, in recruitment, we're in a war all right, a war of the minds. We're in a constant battle for the attention of our prospects, to persuade candidates to work with *us*, not them; we're turning up to events trying to get the most face time with clients, knowing our competition will be there with the same goal.

To reach the top of our industry, become a high performer and hopefully a top biller, we should be waking every day with a warlike mentality, to win the battles of each day. If you know that your main competition gets into their office earlier than you, then you know you will need to open the laptop from home or get up earlier.

When we know that our competition falls down in a specific area, when we are given that opportunity to book a meeting with a prospect, we will do so with confidence, because we know, for a fact, that we can add more value. We will post on LinkedIn regularly and win the war of attention, because we have more success stories and a better understanding of how we operate, and potential clients will want to see our content, and not the competition's.

But how can we win the daily battles of recruitment, and life, without knowing our competition inside and out? We will often see people we compete against at networking events, at industry awards events or maybe even out in public, working hours or not. Get to know them. Not in a weird, creepy and narcissistic way, but just as you would when getting to know anyone. Find out what makes them tick. How they are finding the market. Their long-term goals. Do they communicate well? Are they shy? Are they ambitious? The list is endless.

You never know, you could also pick up a new friend along the way; I know I have. A short-sighted view would be to look at this person as an enemy full stop; the longer you spend in your recruitment career the more you'll realise not everyone is an enemy forever. Times change, people change and companies restructure. How do you know that, five years down the line, you won't set up your own business and need to recruit the best recruiters? What a feeling to know you've already befriended every recruiter in your market and know who's shit hot, and who's not.

Tip Fifteen
Get Specific with Your Calling Times

*'The bad news is time flies.
The good news is you're the pilot.'*
Michael Altshuler, American entrepreneur, author
and motivational speaker

We're a few tips in now, and we're about to move up a gear. This next one could be considered micro niche, but it has allowed me to nurture long-lasting professional relationships with candidates and clients. Specifically, it's the recommendation to call someone at exactly the time you've agreed, on the minute, and not a second before or after.

If you're someone who does this already, then you're well on your way to the top. It's clear to me, without knowing you, that you are organised and respect people's time, two traits that will indeed allow you to excel in recruitment. If you don't do this, it may seem militant and unrealistic. I mean, so what if you're calling someone at 14:02 instead of 14:00? What's a couple of minutes in someone's day? but I need to remind you about the power of words.

Most of us humans take words at face value, and if I'm expecting a call at 14:00, I'm waiting by my phone at 14:00.

I can't tell you how many times candidates have thanked me over the years for calling them at the exact time we agreed. They've shared stories from other recruiters being up to thirty minutes late, and some completely missing the call. We only get one chance to create a first impression, and less than a handful of times to establish credibility with an individual. People are busy, and a few minutes here and there can make all the difference.

Let's work through a typical example of how you may approach a scheduled call. You've agreed to call Tom at 12:00pm when his lunchbreak starts. Tom's a senior accountant and you've been waiting nearly a week to speak to him about an opportunity. Unknowingly to you, Tom also has three other calls scheduled in his lunch break and luckily has prioritised you as the first person to speak with.

What's the most common approach here? Opening up his CV at 11:58 to read through, calling him at 12:05 because you took too long getting a coffee? Besides running the risk of Tom speaking to someone else before you, you've also now created the perception that you don't value your own, or his, time. I don't need to tell you that this is an unorganised, sloppy approach to recruitment, and if you choose to allow yourself to behave like this, your market share will get eaten by your competition.

Ideally, you'll have found time to digest and review somebody's CV before the day of actually speaking to them, but as we know, recruitment can be a busy, demanding industry. Even so, taking fifteen minutes before an arranged call to read through their CV is vital. I'm old school, so where possible I'll

Get Specific with Your Calling Times | 67

have their CV printed with certain areas highlighted and notes attached to the page, usually sticky notes. I'm sure it's a more productive use of time to do this online now, but you get the gist. Make sure you've prepared two or three thought-provoking questions to really show the candidate you've taken the time to understand their story. It's no exaggeration when I say that, at 11:59, I'll have the person's number on my phone ready to hit dial at 12:00. Some, maybe even the majority of you might think this is extreme, but it creates a lasting impact on whoever you're speaking to.

There are hundreds if not thousands of recruiters operating in the exact same market as you do. That often means a handful of recruiters fighting for the attention and respect of a single candidate. We get one single opportunity for a first impression, and a few opportunities to prove to people that we're credible. That we're on the ball. That we're someone worth speaking to. How we do this is by sweating the small stuff, by calling people at the exact time we say we will, by doing exactly what we said we'd do.

If you're early on in your recruitment career, you may, like most of us, be encountering self-doubt and some imposter syndrome. After all, why would a senior manager of a multi-million-pound business want to speak with a junior recruiter? Don't worry yourself, because you have a chance to punch above your weight by sweating the small stuff.

You may be familiar with Viktor Frankl, the Auschwitz survivor and Austrian psychiatrist, who famously said 'control the controllables'. It's a quote that resonates with the recruitment industry greatly. The only things we can control are our actions and inputs, which in turn creates a perception in others. We must never forget that the recruitment industry is growing, and our competition is most likely improving, so if we're not building better habits and moving forward, we're falling behind. There are recruiters out there constantly making small improvements, continuing to win new clients and strengthen their relationships. In other words, they're sweating the small stuff, the stuff that, over time, results in big changes.

Tip Sixteen
Develop a Growth Mindset Over a Fixed One

'You have to apply yourself each day to becoming a little better. By becoming a little better each and every day, over a period of time, you will become a lot better.'
John Wooden, American basketball coach

Neuroscience and psychology are two topics that truly fascinate me. The brain is incredibly complex, but when we start to understand how it works and why it does certain things, we can use our brain power to program itself into more efficient thinking and doing. Now is probably a good time to state the obvious and tell you I'm not currently qualified in either of these domains. But I have a keen interest in them, have read and listened to over seventy books on various topics of human physiology, and most importantly I have a healthy amount of life experience in trying new things, failure and pushing my own limits. Everything I share in this topic will be from personal experience, and if this topic piques your interest, I'd encourage you to look deeper into neuroscience, NLP and psychology to see how they're able to benefit your recruitment career.

Would you believe me if I told you that our childhood and upbringing has almost certainly affected the way we operate on a daily basis, consciously and subconsciously? Interactions with our parents, teachers and closest peers in our most important developmental years have an ongoing impact on our approach to life. Thanks to Carol Dweck and her magnificent book *Mindset*, this area of self-improvement has gained momentum over the last few years and is now in the mainstream.

It goes without saying that I encourage you to read the book, as well as to use Google to search the topic of growth mindset, where you'll find many articles, books and live talks. That being said, I'd like to give you a simplified explanation. People who choose a growth mindset have accepted that all of their abilities and skills can be developed through hard work and dedication. On the other hand, a fixed mindset is where someone has chosen to believe that their talents and personal traits cannot be improved. People with a fixed mindset are of the opinion that, no matter how hard you work or how much effort you put in, you cannot improve on the abilities you were born with. This often means that if they're not good at something, they don't try to improve themselves in that area.

As someone who has actively chosen a growth mindset over time and consciously striven to improve my natural thought processes, to me it sounds preposterous to think we cannot improve on the foundations we have been given. Imagine some things you're relatively good at – I'll use football

Develop a Growth Mindset | 71

as an example – and give your current skill level an honest rating out of ten. If you said ten, you're definitely a recruiter. But assuming you're not Kylian Mbappé fancying a career change, let's say that realistically you're a five or a six. Now let's pretend that you're willing to invest the next five years to see if you can improve in this area. You hire a one-on-one coach, join a competitive team, train once a week and play a match on the weekend. You study footage of some of the footballing greats, read their books, watch their greatest goals and try to develop a footballing brain. Do you *really* believe, after five years of such dedication, that you wouldn't improve as a footballer? I find that hard to accept. But people really do believe this.

It's an attitude often taught to us at a young age and carried subconsciously through to our adult life. I'd like to share two simple examples of how our parents may have unknowingly pushed us in the direction of a fixed mindset, through no fault of their own. Think back to when you were a child: were you way above average in a subject? Let's use Maths as an example. Constant reassurances and praise that you're 'so talented' and 'it just comes naturally to you' can seriously hinder you from putting in any extra effort to improve on your ability. I mean, why improve in an area you're blessed in already? But say you're also struggling in Science. Conversely, phrases like 'maybe science just isn't for you' or 'it's OK, you can't be good at everything, let's play to your strengths' will encourage you to only focus on tasks you're good at. Whilst it may be true that Science is not a natural strength, that doesn't mean that our abilities can't be improved. How counterintuitive is it to admit to ourselves we're just not good in an area, so we'll avoid practicing it altogether? I hope you can now appreciate the perspective of adopting a growth mindset.

But now let's focus on recruitment. Recruitment is unquestionably a profession that requires us to have a growth mindset, to regularly improve our communication skills and train ourselves in the latest technologies and tools that become available to us. The ability to ask the right questions when speaking to candidates, the confidence to push back on objections when calling prospects and marketing our online personal brand are all skills that can be taught. Find me someone who was born good at cold calling and I'll refund you this book. It's a load of codswallop. Cold calling is a skill that every single person can, and should, improve on. How many different ways can you think of that would help improve your cold calling? Listening back to your calls and making notes, roleplaying with your colleagues, hiring a one-on-one coach, attending bootcamps, watching YouTube videos on other people cold calling. And how about, wait for it… actually cold calling yourself. You're going to fail way more than you succeed when it comes to cold calling. You're going to get the phone put down on you, some people will hurl abuse at you, and there are certain people who might actually report you (I actually know someone who had a serious complaint for the amount of poor cold calls made to an individual). But even with all the negativity you may experience, cold calling with a growth mindset will give you the perspective that every call is a learning opportunity. Each call is a chance to marginally improve, improvements which compound over time. With a growth mindset, your training and learning are never complete, and there is always an opportunity to improve in any area you desire. This is fundamental to achieving high performance.

Tip Seventeen
Invest in Your Own Personal Development

*'Investing in yourself is the most important
investment you'll ever make in your life.'*
Tim Ferris, American entrepreneur, author and investor

Personal development should not be seen as a cost but an investment. Investment in ourselves is essentially putting time and/or money into something, like a course or a coach, that we expect to turn a profit, or provide a positive outcome, at a later date. The key words to highlight there are 'at a later date'.

Throughout my recruitment career, there's not a lot I regret. I just don't think of past experiences like that. But thinking back on my earlier years in recruitment, if there was one area that I could go back and change it would be my outlook on paying for my own career and personal development. There were a number of occasions over the years when I may have had the opportunity to learn something new or further develop a certain area, but like most I would always expect my employer to front the cost. If they were also to experience the benefits, then surely they should foot the bill?

Hindsight is a wonderful thing. I couldn't have been more wrong. I wasn't really taking a stand: it was simply a price-motivated decision. I didn't step back and consider the long-term benefits of investing in my own development.

To be fair, there are times when an employer should, and probably would, pay for your training and development. Let's imagine our employer is suggesting and offering us the opportunity to take on more responsibility, which could be a promotion to a senior management position. Most employers, at least in my personal experience, would be happy to support us through this transition with extra training. It's not unusual for companies to hire external group trainers, one-to-one mentors, or even pay for full-day offsite training with a specialist. Understandably, if we have achieved a promotion which puts more weight on our shoulders, we should always look to take our employer up on this offer.

However, there are other times when you know you might need to improve on a skill, and doing so will take you up another level as a recruiter. We're talking about being the best we can be here: at the end of the day, that's our own responsibility.

I expect there will be recruiters at all levels reading this book, and regardless of your incredible billings or your length of service to the industry, it's never too late, or early, to invest in ourselves. What opportunities for personal and career development did I potentially miss out on because of my reluctance to put my hand in my own pocket? To name a few, there was sales training with an individual and groups, seminars with mentors I admired, network groups that hosted

Invest in Your Personal Development | 75

regular meetups, one-to-one coaches I might have hired, digital training platforms that provided monthly content, online webinars from key trainers, and last but not least, books I might have read (I really do hope you don't mind paying for your own books though).

The quicker we accept that our career development is in our own hands, the better and more successful career we will achieve. There are quite literally hundreds of different ways to facilitate your development in this modern era. Gone are the days when we needed to physically turn up to a certain location, on a set day, to gain from a course or program. We're now able to attend meetings with our business coach via online video call; we can read books anywhere in the world; we can listen to audiobooks and podcasts in our cars; we can even complete a training course on a digital platform on our phone, whenever we can make the time. I believe personal development has never been more accessible than it is today. Not only is it available, but it's actually seen as *cool* to be into personal development, at least that's my perspective. I truly hope it continues on this upward trajectory for years to come.

There are individuals who have lived similar professional lives to us, walked along similar journeys, and share similar battle scars. And some of them are willing to give back to people, supporting them on their own journeys too. If you're considering where you could start investing in yourself, a mentor or personal coach such as these would be a great start.

Let's not hide the fact that recruitment pays well, and throughout your career most of you will experience some big commissions (hopefully after reading this book). A mindset I've now incorporated is to spend a minimum of 10% of my commissions on personal development. I'd encourage you to do the same. If you're in a position where you have low outgoings (if you're still living with your parents perhaps), why not make it 20% or 30%? Spending your own hard-earned money on improving yourself is an investment that you'll never regret. But remember, investing time or money means expecting a return at a *later date,* so don't expect to hire a sales trainer and start winning new business the following day. If you do, send me that trainer's number, please. I'm asking for a colleague.

Tip Eighteen
Make Networking a Priority

'The single greatest "people skill" is a highly developed and authentic interest in the other person.'
Bob Burg, American author and speaker

It's no secret that the connections we have and the relationships we build have a direct impact on our financial success, overall wealth and our eminence in our chosen career. Simply put, our network is our net worth. In the course of our careers, we will sometimes need to call in favours, or to lean on senior figures for advice; occasionally we may also have the opportunity to connect two individuals who would greatly benefit from knowing each other.

Everyone you ever meet knows something that you don't, and networking allows us access to this knowledge, as well as the chance to embrace new ideas. Not only this, but as I was told as a young recruiter, each person we meet will have access to two individual people who could impact our professional lives for the better. Across my career, I have found that piece of wisdom to be true.

When I first started in recruitment, I had a very short-sighted approach to networking. When I say short-sighted, I don't mean that I would deceive people; I have always understood the power of strong relationships, both professionally and personally. I mean that I didn't consider the future: how in three, five, or even twenty years' time, my network might develop, grow and support my career.

It can sometimes be hard to imagine that a candidate you're representing, let's say a graduate software developer, might go on to be a manager of some sort, responsible for hiring into a team; it's harder still to think that, in ten more years, perhaps, they'll be an executive member of a board. But time goes on and circumstances change. This is something to remember when speaking to, say, a senior manager who's out of work and having a tough time looking for their next opportunity; we might not have anything for them right now, but that doesn't mean we can't offer our advice and support them in their search, or even meet them for a coffee to hear about their journey.

The best way to connect with industry leaders and professionals is in-person networking events. There are a number of events hosted on a monthly basis, no matter what industry you're in. Websites like MeetUp and EventBrite provide regular email updates on the latest events in your area. If you're working in education recruitment, for example, it would make sense to attend events about the various micro-niches of the education industry, but why not also attend other networking events that take your interest, like business, entrepreneurship events, or events with famous guest-speakers? There are bound to be invaluable people at all of them.

Make Networking a Priority | 79

Bob Burg is a bestselling author who talks a lot of sense, mostly around influence and authority marketing. Two quotes of his really summarise what networking is all about; the first is at the top of this tip and the second is as follows: 'The successful networkers I know, the ones receiving tons of referrals and feeling truly happy about themselves, continually put the other person's needs ahead of their own.'

Networking should be seen as a time to give and learn about others. To get the most out of networking, we need to be proving value, not expecting favours. Becoming truly invested in other people's journeys is a skill that takes a long time to master, but time spent developing good listening skills and a genuine curiosity for other people is well worth it. If you've not yet attended a networking event, I'll let you into a secret (and if you have, you'll know exactly what I mean here): there is nothing more alienating than someone who only talks about themselves and barely asks a question about you.

Attending networking events can be daunting, particularly if you plan to attend on your own, so it's beneficial to attend with someone if possible. At first, most people will attend with colleagues, because realistically these are the easiest people to ask to join you. However, as your network grows, you might want to reach out to clients, or even candidates. It's a great way to strengthen any business relationship.

That way, you'll have a warm introduction to any of their connections at the event, and vice versa. Once you're comfortable with networking events and have attended your fair share, you'll likely recognise the regulars and be able to decide who you should prioritise building relationships with.

Depending on the industry you work in, you may yourself decide to host your own professional networking events. I know this is really prominent in tech and finance. It's a great idea and a seriously impressive way to attract the most influential leaders in your industry. That said, I can only see it being feasible once you are well-established in your industry, or at least working for an established company. It will likely require a team effort, a strategic approach and an already-strong network to get up and running.

Networking events are fun, and the possibilities are endless, but there's no denying they can be exhausting too. At the end of a difficult day or a long week, going to an event booked the week before might be the last thing we want to do. As Herminia Ibarra – the bestselling author and professor at London Business School - once said, 'Networking is a lot like nutrition and fitness: we know what to do, the hard part is making it a top priority.' Doesn't that hold some weight? We know we should be doing it, but it's hard to motivate ourselves sometimes.

I'd like to close this tip with some short, quick-fire pieces of advice that I've absorbed from attending countless events, in the hope of helping you find the umph to attend an event. When you walk into any event, be confident – even if you're dying inside – and smile at everyone you get the opportunity to. There's no better way to initiate a conversation than a heart-warming smile. If you're alone, which is totally fine, get yourself a drink and walk up to someone else who's also attended alone, and start a conversation. It's highly likely that your competition will also be at an industry event, and I'd always recommend saying hello and taking an interest in them. Finally, keep in mind that networking is about giving value and connecting with people. If you have the opportunity to introduce someone to one of your connections, do it. The more you give, the more you'll receive, but it's not about keeping score.

Tip Nineteen
Always Provide Value, Don't Be a Vulture

'Strive not to be a success, but rather to be of value.'
Albert Einstein, German-born theoretical physicist

Vultures are interesting creatures. I know you didn't decide to read this book for a lesson on birds of prey, but here we are. Vultures are scavengers that prey on the weak, but they're an important part of our ecosystem. In the world of recruitment, however, having vulture-like tendencies won't serve you in the long term. A recruitment vulture is a contemptible individual who looks to exploit others and has their own personal interests at the forefront of their intentions.

The opposite of a vulture would be someone who actively goes out of their way to provide value, before expecting anything in return. They're not patiently waiting to pounce on the next hiring manager or candidate, but rather proactively looking for ways to support others. There are various ways we can support others: through advice, guidance, introductions, referrals, discounts or even gifts.

You might recognise I'm a fan of Bob Burg, and his fantastic book *The Go-Giver* is a good read for anyone in recruitment. Forgive me for quoting Bob again, but on the topics of networking and providing value, none others come close, in my opinion. The following resonates with me to this day: 'Your true worth is determined by how much more you give in value than you take in payment.' I don't think it's a surprise that some of the most successful people in your industry are likely following the same principles of *The Go-Giver*.

Sadly, a lot of recruiters are sick with MCS – main character syndrome – and often put their own needs first, constantly digging for what's in it for them. The modern phenomenon of MCS is ripe in the recruitment industry, and it shows in many interactions between recruiters and hiring managers. Recruiters will call a hiring manager every month simply to talk about recruitment. When are they hiring? What are they hiring? Can they help with the hiring? They can also fall guilty of calling candidates and extracting leads, promising callbacks with no opportunities and so on. With such recruiters, it is too often a one-way street.

Despite all the mouthwash available on the market, I've not yet seen a brand that is capable of curing a severe case of a recruiter's commission breath. Hiring managers can smell it through the phone. You might recognise the whiff of it too, from those times when all we do is talk about jobs and recruitment after not speaking to a client for six months. It's no surprise that candidates, too, can smell our commission breath, when we regularly call to pull leads with no opportunities, or manipulate them into thinking a vacancy we have is the best on the market, knowing full well it's not.

Providing value is a mindset shift that takes some effort.

Always Provide Value, Don't Be a Vulture | 83

But there are a few areas in recruitment that you'll experience routinely and that are the perfect times to practice.

There's the period of time between a company finishing their most recent recruitment drive and starting their next, which is the perfect opportunity to showcase that you know the market and understand the company's world. While a lot of recruiters will tactically call every few weeks for 'updates' that suit them, why not instead call to provide insights into the market? Are they aware of the salary increases in a specific niche that will affect them when they do hire? How about a competitor making 20% of their workforce redundant due to a lack of sales? Even a new technology or tool that you think might benefit their business because someone has referred it to you, or their competition speaks highly about the tools.

When it comes to speaking with candidates, long-term relationships are crucial for long-term success, and you can't build a long-term relationship without trust. When speaking to candidates regularly, you'll notice that some are happy to share information about their current job search, and some aren't. Either way, the more value we can give, the better relationships we can build. If we don't have any opportunities for them, why not point them in the direction of a company hiring? There will be times when a candidate will have an interview with a company we work with, either directly or through a competitor agency; why not let them know they're a good employer? Alternatively, on occasion we'll speak to people who aren't selling their skills effectively; offering some advice and guidance on their CV will be remembered for a long time.

I have no doubts that all of you reading this will have been on the receiving end of insincere kindness and support from someone. It can be bleedingly obvious. So make sure you're genuinely acting selflessly, expecting nothing in return. Being an individual who provides value to other people starts as a mentality shift but will turn into a way of life once you experience the benefits of helping others. I'd go as far as saying it's an addiction – a positive one of course!

I'm not just talking about helping hiring managers and candidates, but our colleagues, the unknown people who we meet at networking events, and while we're at it, why not the cleaner or receptionist? We are all so caught up in the turbulence of our own lives that we can forget the power of giving to others, and how it creates a ripple effect in the universe. Often an act of kindness will be passed on by the recipient, and so on.

An example that has served me well over the years, particularly when working with colleagues, is sharing market insights. By showing a genuine interest in colleagues and their recruitment needs, I've been able to share candidates that might be looking for new opportunities, passed on information of a company looking to make redundancies, and of a company actively hiring but using a competitor. Then there's been times when I've booked a meeting with a prospective client and invited a colleague for experience and the opportunity to cross sell.

As an avid networker, I've learnt over time there is a golden rule for becoming a *good* networker, and that's when you realise the true power is in giving, not receiving. The people who are held in the highest regard in the networking communities are those that give the most – funny that, isn't it?

Whether you believe in karma or not is not the point; I can wholeheartedly tell you that what goes around comes around.

Always Provide Value, Don't Be a Vulture | 85

Even better than that, the energy and value we put out into the world comes back tenfold. It will take time, but if you can acquire the outlook of providing value before asking for anything in return, your network will grow and opportunities multiply. And if you're a vulture looking for a quick kill... Well, they're unpopular birds for a reason.

Tip Twenty
Get Good at Writing Job Adverts

'Write the way you talk. Naturally.'
David Ogilvy, British advertising tycoon

Sales calls, networking, working outside of core hours, counter offers, emails, LinkedIn branding… These are all things we accept as part of our responsibilities as recruiters. But creative writing? For many of you, that's probably the last thing you think of when you picture the fast-paced world of recruitment. Yet isn't effectively writing job adverts part of our list of core responsibilities, too? In which case, wouldn't it make sense to write the most compelling adverts possible: adverts which work in the background to attract talent whilst you focus on more selling?

To start us off, think about a job advert in the traditional sense, such as you might see posted by a company recruiting organically using Indeed, Reed or LinkedIn. Are the adverts they typically post easy on the eye? What words do they use? How long are they? More importantly, why do they all look the

Get Good at Writing Job Adverts | 87

same? I imagine that 90% of job adverts posted directly follow a similar format. Without a doubt, it's always an *exciting* time to join a *forward-thinking company* that is likely experiencing some *growth*. You'll notice companies that have a high turnover rate still use words like *growth* and *huge pipeline,* even though they're most likely backfilling five positions.

They then usually move on to a paragraph about the company, when they were founded, who they are and what they do. What I can say for certain is that no one – and I mean no one – is deciding to interview at a company because of this paragraph. Unless a company is completely revolutionising an industry or doing something remarkably interesting, it's probably doing more harm than good.

Then right on cue, there's a section of bullet points that share the responsibilities and essential criteria for the job. Points like '*must be able to work in a fast-paced environment*' – what does that even mean anymore? Probably that they're understaffed and will need you to work longer hours if you can't keep up. They may also tell you that you need to tick ten '*non-negotiable*' criteria, like having a university degree from a top university and six years' experience with a certain tool. In my experience, companies don't actually require a university degree and would consider someone with three years' experience, providing they had the right attitude. Sounds contradictory, right?

These job advert formats have been consistently followed for years – longer than I've been in recruitment, and probably longer than I've actually been old enough to work. I'll put my neck on the line and say they are outdated, lack creativity and don't target the right candidates. It's no wonder companies need to use agencies.

I'm sure you're thinking, well how else should we write an advert then? And that's a good question. To start with, ditch the script. We are now writing adverts to be viewed by different generations all at the same time: some may be at the end of their career and looking for something specific, some may be newly entering the workforce and may (just may) have shorter attention spans. If any company are looking to hire gen z, for example, these old adverts aren't going to cut it.

To write better adverts, we need to take better job briefs. We need to ask better questions to uncover some truths about the vacancy. Most of our work as recruiters will be headhunting, and companies will always prioritise someone who has relevant industry experience or similar qualifications. That should get us thinking. Why would someone in the same role in the same industry move to a competitor?

Let's look at a few examples. If the company you're recruiting for offers career progression opportunities and has a track record of fast-track promoting the right people, it will appeal to someone who is ambitious but doesn't have opportunities for promotion at their current company. Or say you are working with a startup or a company in its infancy: a hiring manager may tell you that a candidate will be expected to 'wear multiple hats', shouldering responsibilities that fall outside of their core job description. Whilst some people may see this as a negative, there will be others currently in roles where they have no or little room for growth who feel unchallenged by their mundane tasks.

Once we know the most interesting areas of a role, we should lead with them in our job adverts. It's not about us; it's not even about the company we're recruiting for. There's no need to start with '*We have partnered with an innovative mar-*

ket-leading tech company', or '*a great opportunity with brilliant progression'*. It's about your audience: who they are and what they want.

If we're looking for a digital marketing executive who's recently graduated, our terminology, references and format will be completely different to if we're looking for a senior quantity surveyor at a construction company. The young digital marketing executive will want to know what their training will be like, who they'll be working with and what channels they will be using for marketing. We could most likely use short, informal sentences to catch their attention. We might also reference some industry trends. On the other hand, a manager whose experience is at a senior level in a construction company will want to know about career progression opportunities, the projects that said company will be working on, and the accuracy and success of some of their recent projects. The terminology we use in an advert aimed at quantity surveyors may be more formal and statistics-based, for example.

I'll leave you with a few non-negotiables when it comes to writing your next job advert. Firstly, it's all about your audience, so use words like 'you' rather than 'I' or 'we'. The idea is to get the reader to move from their current dissatisfied state to thinking about the state we are offering; we can do that with phrases like 'can you imagine', 'what would you do' or 'are you someone'. In the wise words of David Ogilvy, just drop the corporate talk. We don't need to use words like 'fast-paced', 'innovative', 'forward-thinking', 'family-oriented' or 'market-leading', to name a few. We need to write how we speak, so it's not only easier for the reader, but quicker too. Which brings me on to length: the shorter we can get our adverts, the better. Writing in one or two lines rather than paragraphs is a great start. Last but absolutely not least: include the salary ranges in the job advert!

The bar for job adverts is at an all-time low. A bit of creativity will help you stand out from the crowd and attract better talent. For anyone on LinkedIn – which I would expect to be every single one of you – you need to follow Mitch Sullivan, if you're not already. He's doing some great work with his company copywritingforrecruiters.com and trying to change the industry for the better.

Tip Twenty-One
Physical Health Will Get You to the Top and Keep You There

'A year from now, you will wish you started today.'
Karen Lamb, Australian teacher and editor

Looking after our physical health is the foundation of success in every other area of our lives. As a person who has prioritised physical activity my whole life, I may be biased with this attitude, but after experiencing all the benefits that have directly impacted my recruitment career for the better, I think it's only fair this tip makes this book.

So we're all on the same page, we're talking about *all* aspects of physical health: both exercise and diet. I covered having a healthy lunch earlier in this book, which allows us to be more productive with our energy and to win the day, but here we'll cover the benefits of an all-round healthy lifestyle.

As a disclaimer, I have no formal qualifications when it comes to fitness or nutrition (unless you count my level three personal training course that I completed at seventeen, before

I decided not to be a PT so I'll keep to a high-level overview to save my getting in trouble with the fitness police. I would like to think that most of you reading will be familiar with the term endorphins. Our bodies release endorphins and one of the biggest releases we get is when we exercise. Releasing these endorphins can help reduce stress, relieve pain and improve our wellbeing.

A regular, structured exercise routine will have us feeling more energised, increasing our productivity and allowing us deeper sleep to support our recovery, empower us to have more focus at work, a higher attention to detail and a willingness to push through when times get tough. Ideally, we should then be able to communicate more efficiently and build better, longer-lasting relationships with both clients and candidates. Isn't it crazy to think you can improve in so many areas by just exercising regularly?

Let's be honest, recruitment *isn't* a physically demanding job, but that shouldn't affect our approach to a healthy lifestyle. In fact, I'd argue that prioritising our physical health is even *more* important because of the lack of movement our job involves. Sitting down for upwards of eight hours a day, five days a week, over many years, will eventually catch up on us. Those 'irregular' snacks that we have once a day might not make a difference in the short term, but they too compound over time.

For me, working out in the morning before work is sacrosanct. Some of you might not be willing to sacrifice the extra time in bed in the morning – I feel you by the way – and that's not a problem, but I would encourage you to make the effort either at lunchtime or in the evening. For anyone that already exercises regularly, I'm sure you can agree that it's near impos-

Physical Health Will Get You to the Top

sible to feel bad after completing some exercise. Sure, beforehand we might feel tired, exhausted or just not in the mood, but it is these moments when you ultimately choose the hard thing that propel you forward.

Often the importance of taking care of our body doesn't become apparent until it's too late, after we start to see signs of physical decline in ourselves. Someone in their early twenties might not experience some of the negative consequences of poor health choices because of faster recovery, a faster metabolism and more natural energy. But by their late twenties they will start to notice the signs that they have been neglecting their health: an increase in chances of illness and disease, weight gain, or postural problems from sitting down in awkward positions for too long. Believe me, no one wants lower back pains at thirty! Not only because of the physical pain, but the financial cost of getting regular treatment too.

Our diet goes hand in hand with exercise and should also be a priority for anyone looking to perform to the best of their ability each day. Eating the right foods at the right time will give us access to consistent energy throughout the day, allowing us to really excel in our responsibilities. Everyone has a unique relationship to the foods they eat, and at what time, so it's best to find out what works for you. What is important to all of us is the intake of the right nutrients, vitamins and minerals.

Physical health is a never-ending process, and it might be comforting for you to know that (within reason) it's never too late to make the decision to start. Anyone who is at the top of their game in any industry will very likely prioritise their health. I encourage you to look at your idols, role models and mentors, particularly in business; I think you'll find the top one percent have dialled in on their nutrition, diet and fitness.

Every piece of exercise we do, and every nutritious meal we eat, is an investment in our future self. It may require us to invest more time, potentially invest more money, in the short term, but the long-term benefits speak for themselves.

In my opinion, the hustle mentality of working ourselves into the ground in a very mentally demanding industry with no care for our health is counterintuitive. What good is it to be financially wealthy but unable to enjoy the luxuries money can provide? There may be times in the future when we want to play some sport, attend Pilates or play with our children. Wouldn't it feel good to be a well-rounded human who earns good money, is physically fit and gives value to others? I think so.

Tip Twenty-Two
Take Your Mental Health Seriously

*'Your mental health is everything – prioritise it.
Make the time like your life depends on it, because it does.'*
Mel Robbins, American broadcaster and author

To master the skill that is recruitment, we first have to master ourselves, to allow ourselves to flourish in the four main pillars of health: physical, mental, social and spiritual. This chapter looks at the fourth of these, the one that many of us neglect. Our spiritual and mental health are just as important as our physical health and should receive our time and attention with the same priority. Luckily, we now live in a world where mental health is taken seriously and supported by others.

Recruitment, like most other sales occupations, is a primarily office-based career. This means that, when we turn up for work in the morning, we don't really risk any of the major negative consequences that might happen on, say, a construction site, where physical strain and exhaustion are common, and workplace accidents can involve serious injury. Whilst us recruiters aren't regularly pushed to our boundaries physically, there's no denying we're constantly pushed to the limits mentally, and if we don't accept the genuine dangers of ignoring our mental health, we run the risk of serious consequences.

As someone who has been unfortunate enough to experience severe burnout, I can assure you it's not something I would ever like to face again. I've always been someone who looked after my physical health, and I thought I had the same endearment when it came to my mental health. But after an episode of burnout it was apparent I didn't. After some reflection, I realised my experience was a blessing in disguise, something I needed to experience to come out stronger on the other end. Being confronted with something like burnout allows you to recognise the signs of mental health neglect in the future.

There are many words I would use to describe the world of recruitment and almost all of them would be positive. But despite all the benefits of working in this industry, it can be a cruel world at times. There is a small percentage of recruiters out there that give the industry a bad name, and while most recruiters come into the industry with positive intentions and clean hearts, people are individually unique and unpredictable, and human behaviour is complex and nebulous at the best of times.

If you've decided on a career in recruitment, congratulations on choosing a profession that is guaranteed to service you more losses than wins. You see, there are not many companies or job seekers that truly enjoy the recruitment process. At first, companies are usually excited when it's time to recruit, because it's generally a result of growth, but they're often met

Take Your Mental Health Seriously | 97

with disappointment and frustration when it comes to the process itself. Having invested time and money, these companies are forced to watch as candidates accept other offers. Then they have to reckon with some harsh truths: they may be paying under the market rate and can't hire the talent they need. Usually, the recruiter facilitating the process is the first person to blame here.

On the other hand, candidates and jobseekers generally dislike the recruitment process from the start, and rightfully so. Think back to times when you have been job searching. How did it go? How did you feel? Were you successful? I'm sure I can speak for most of us when I say that searching for a new job is mentally tiring, and sometimes physically tiring too. Candidates need to be as flexible as possible to accommodate the needs of companies, sometimes investing hours of their own time to prepare for each interview. They are commonly asked to complete technical assessments or presentations in their own time. Who in their right mind would enjoy spending hours of their own time working unpaid for multiple different companies, sometimes with no income coming in whilst they're doing so? Again, despite our best intentions, recruiters usually take the brunt of any disappointment and frustration.

That brings us nicely on to us recruiters and why we can often be left short. I wholeheartedly believe that if the people on either side of the process – candidates and hiring managers – could spend a week in a recruiter's shoes, they would change their perspective on the whole industry. The amount of time, effort and support invested on a daily basis to help both candidates find their dream roles and companies the best talent is regularly overlooked by both parties.

Despite our good intentions and genuine desire to support

people and businesses improve their processes, we're almost guaranteed to encounter regular setbacks: candidates telling you they haven't been represented by another agency for a role, only for it then to turn out they have; hiring managers lecturing you on how important a role is, only for it to be withdrawn from the market two days later; your favourite customer going through an acquisition process, which leads to a new in-house team for recruitment; a candidate you've worked hard to get a new opportunity accepting a different offer at the last minute, or worse a counter offer; and the worst of all, a candidate who's accepted the offer for a new opportunity with you only to drop out the day before they're due to start. This is a small list of an endless number of possibilities that can completely throw off your day and week.

With the next rejection or setback always on the horizon, it's important to be kind to yourself and to your team members. Open communication and collaboration are fundamental to a high-performance culture, a culture that supports in the face of setbacks and failures, and encourages individuals to move forward stronger. It's paramount to understand that with big losses come big wins, so when you're going through a rough patch, just know there are brighter days ahead.

Tip Twenty-Three
Asking Better Questions Produces Better Answers

'The smart ones ask when they don't know.
And sometimes, they ask when they do.'
Malcolm Forbes, former New Jersey state senator

Do you think it's possible to ask the perfect question every time? Well, maybe not. But we can get consistently *good* at asking the right questions at the right time. And it's crucial that we do. One of the most important attributes we need as a recruiter is curiosity, and with curiosity comes questions.

What was your answer to the question by the way? It was likely a yes or a no, and that's because my question was a very basic example of a closed question in action. Close-ended questions usually require short, direct answers, so they are often frowned upon. But they do serve a purpose. There is a time and a place to obtain quantitative data. 'Is the maximum salary £35,000 for this role?' 'What is the bonus structure?' 'Would you hire a junior for this role?' These are examples of close-ended questions which have a limited number of possible answers, usually no more than a word or two.

Yet, in the world of recruitment, you will often hear that closed questions are our worst enemy, and it's true that we frequently ask them because of a lack of preparation, understanding or curiosity. I've been responsible for asking many closed questions, and it takes some serious thinking and behavioural changes to adjust them to more well-constructed questions that enable us to gather better information. Closed questions will often start with words like 'did', 'was' or 'is', and they will generally shut down a conversation quickly. Asking a hiring manager something like 'Is this role for a senior?' will only prompt a short answer, probably yes or no. If we can reframe this question to 'What are your expectations in terms of seniority for this position?', it requires a more open response, and we are more likely to hear the truth.

Like I said, closed questions have a time and a place in recruitment, but they often leave us coming up short. The worst examples are what are known as double-ended or double-barrelled questions. These are essentially two questions at once: 'So, Mrs Hiring Manager, what do you think the most important qualification is for the candidate to have? Is it the CIPD or the FirstAid?' or 'Mr Hiring Manager, what is the reason for the hire? Is it a backfill or a new position in the business?' Nine times out of ten the speaker will pick one of those two options. Double-ended questions are common across the board in recruitment, and I personally think it comes down to a lack of confidence. Recruiters, especially those in the first few years of learning the profession, just can't resist offering up options. We often just don't have the confidence to ask a well thought out question and zip it to wait for the answer.

Here's another example: 'So, Mrs Candidate, why are you looking for a new role? Is it because of your salary or maybe the career progression opportunities?' How much better if we were to drop the options: 'So, Mr Candidate, why are you looking for a new role?' That's a perfect question to start a conversation with. It's open, meaning there is no set response, so the person will need to think and construct their own response, likely the truth (but not always).

Open-ended questions don't lead someone to a specific answer and won't be answerable with just a yes or no. They allow a person to elaborate on their answer. These questions will typically start with 'Why', 'How', 'What' or 'Tell me about'. These questions work wonders when extracting information from candidates or hiring managers, particularly if they are withholding information for whatever reason. 'Mrs Candidate, tell me about your experience working at x company?' and 'Mr Hiring Manager, can you describe your company culture to me?' are questions that require some thinking and a more detailed answer.

To help us become more consciously aware of when to ask these questions, start practising on your colleagues, friends or even people at home, and make note of how much more information you receive when you ask an open question. Something as basic as 'Are we going to the pub for lunch?' (I see you, certain recruiters) could be rephrased as 'What are you guys thinking for lunch today?'

There is a right time for a closed question, and that's normally when you want a yes or no, or an exact number. Honestly, I don't think there's ever a time for a double-barrelled question, though; they should be eradicated from any recruiter's vocabulary. Open-ended questions are the single best way to gather as much information as possible and also allow the responder to be as honest as possible. As the Malcolm Forbes quote suggests, the smarter the individual, the more questions they will ask, even if they know the answer.

What use is asking a question if you already know the answer, though? Let me explain. Say that you know that two people have resigned and are working a notice period at an organisation. You know this because you've spoken to them personally. You also know that their resignations were because of a bad culture and lack of projects in the pipeline. Our first question to the hiring manager should be a nicely constructed open question such as 'So, Mr Hiring Manager, can you tell me how these roles have come about in the company?'

We already know the answer, but we're testing their honesty, and we'll learn something more about them for how they choose to respond.

Tip Twenty-Four
Build Your Personal Brand Online

'Your brand is what you represent, and what people say about you when you're not in the room.'
Gary Vaynerchuk, American entrepreneur

If you're a gen z or even a gen alpha reading this book, I have no doubts you'll already be well along this journey and probably doing very well. What tips could you possibly take from a dinosaur millennial like me? But don't count me out yet; despite my deciding to build an online brand later in my career, I've reaped some benefits and have come to understand some vital dos and don'ts.

When I started in recruitment, there wasn't *really* a term like personal branding or any particular emphasis placed on building a reputation online. Sure, people were posting on social media occasionally, but I don't think there was a long-term strategy behind the posts, at least not for me anyway.

I'm sure there were some visionaries that knew personal branding would become huge, but sadly I wasn't one of them.

Personal branding always appeared to be a thing somebody did for you, not that you did yourself. Let's take celebrities for example. The press helps build their online personal brand, which in turn helps them become more popular and increase their potential opportunities. It took me some time to realise that, just because they have someone building their brand for them, we can still build our own brands ourselves.

It seems to me that it wasn't until the last ten years or so that personal branding really took off and hit the mainstream. In the last five years we have seen the emergence of hundreds of specialist agencies that solely help people build their online brand. Everyday people like you and me are now seeing the benefits of building an online personal brand to enhance their personal and business opportunities.

There are well over 200,000 recruiters in the UK alone, all of them battling for the same hiring managers' and candidates' attentions. You could say that, with this many recruiters sharing content, as well as approaching the same people, there is an element of intoxication, or information overload. But imagine that two recruiters of exactly equal ability are trying to control the same niche market, say here in sunny Cardiff for example. One of those recruiters posts daily on LinkedIn, and has done so for six months, progressively building up a following by providing value and insights to their target audience. They also regularly attend networking events, have made a guest speaking appearance, and host online webinars about how to write creative job descriptions.

On the other hand, a second recruiter of exactly the same ability has the potential to do all of the above but doesn't. They don't see the benefit of networking or posting online, and rather prioritise sitting at their desk building relationships on

Build Your Personal Brand Online | 105

the phone. They decide not to post on LinkedIn because they struggle to think of original content on a weekly basis, and they're also scared about what their peers or colleagues may think of them. (Top tip, no one cares. People will more than likely be jealous that you have the confidence to post openly.)

Which recruiter do you think will become a more recognised figure in their industry and, in turn, win more new business? When the first candidate makes those sales calls, attends those networking events, creates those daily posts or asks for referrals, they are leveraging their personal brand through omnichannel communications. You can't measure the importance of making the best use of multiple channels. For example, you might get an inbound inquiry on LinkedIn, and you think it's because you regularly share content of value. However, in reality you met the inquirer's business partner at a networking event, hosted a webinar that one of the board members attended, and you cold called them six months ago. Can you now see the effects of omnichannel outreach?

There have been countless times when I have been at a networking event and people have recognised me from posting content (and my face, shamelessly) on LinkedIn. We're not just referring to anyone here, but founders, CEOs, managing directors and senior leaders in business, some of whom have turned into clients and friends. The amount of times I've called either a hiring manager or a candidate, given my name, and they have complimented a thought-provoking post I shared last week, sometimes amazes me.

Best of all, as a result of all this brand building, over time you should be able to experience inbound business inquiries, like candidates looking for new work and choosing to work with you exclusively, or companies showing interest in using your services. Granted, these are rare, but truly rewarding when they happen.

So, how and where do you even start building this online presence? To be honest, we now live in a time where almost every industry micro-niche has professionals, and personal branding is one of them. If you're serious about building your brand for the long term, there are people out in the market who know way more than me. I'd encourage you to speak to them for long-term support.

But to get started, here's a few key areas that you need to get to grips with. Building a brand can be done on all social media platforms, but as a recruiter we should prioritise LinkedIn. A good place to start is to really understand yourself, your service offering and the problems you solve for your potential clients. This will take some time, and the answers might be constantly evolving, so don't feel like you need this nailed in the first week. But once you've got a good understanding, you can begin to communicate your values, your personality and your success stories to your audience.

Posts about your personal life, engaging stories about client wins, and free value and tips are three important areas to cover consistently. Over time, I have no doubts you'll start to enjoy your personal branding efforts. Content will start to come naturally to you, and it will provide an outlet for your creative ideas. Personally, I think you have levelled up your branding game when you truly understand your ICP's (ideal customer profile's) pain points, and you have learned to target your content to help those prospects see that you understand their world, and they can trust you.

Posting on LinkedIn is at minimum a three-day-a-week commitment. You should be posting four or five if you can. Let's face it, starting out with anything in life is tough, and at first it can be really difficult to think of regular content. You'll need to accept that your posts won't always be the hit you expect and some people might not resonate with or enjoy them. Be confident, add value and most importantly be sincere to yourself, and over time things will compound and you will start to see results. If you don't join this journey now, imagine the mountain you'll have to climb in 2030 when everyone else is ten years deep.

Tip Twenty-Five
Strengthen Your Reputation and Protect It at All Costs

'It takes twenty years to build a reputation and five minutes to ruin it. If you think about that, you'll do things differently.'
Warren Buffett, American businessman,
investor and philanthropist

Reputation, what does it mean to you? Is it important to you? Do you care what other people think of you professionally? Are you aware that your day-to-day actions contribute to others' perspectives and how they consider you? To me, the importance of my reputation is unimpeachable; I go out of my way to build, maintain and, most of all, protect it. I believe a strong personal and professional reputation will open doors for new business opportunities, potential career opportunities and professional friendships.

If we consider people who are famous, or at least in the public eye, the first three people I think of who all enjoy a good reputation: Tom Hardy, Daniel Radcliffe and Beyoncé. Some of you may have different opinions, but generally

Strengthen Your Reputation and Protect It at All Costs | 109

speaking, Tom, Daniel and Beyoncé are well-liked individuals considered role models for the younger generation.

Let's flip that to famous people who *haven't* understood the power of their reputation: who've and neglected it through poor decision making. The first three that come to mind for me are Amber Heard, Will Smith and Chris Brown. I'm sure I don't need to go into any detail here to explain *why* these individuals have jeopardised their reputation, but we can see the effects: years of hard work crumbling down through one bad comment or action, whether public or not.

I think most of us will know someone with a strong reputation in our industry. That someone has most likely been in the game for many years, is considered trustworthy and upholds solid core values, but most importantly, their reputation has been built on real accomplishments. Recruiters, particularly high performers and top billers, understand that their reputation is the key to long-term success. They understand the importance of being seen, heard and talked about as an individual who is professional, loyal and results driven. Possessing a reputation as someone who provides results when the odds are stacked against you, someone with excellent communication skills, and knowledge of your industry, will provide countless opportunities: new business opportunities, because people trust you and are willing to refer connections to you; invitations to industry events, whether to attend or as a guest speaker; maybe even life-changing career opportunities in other countries; or the chance to invest in, join or collaborate with a new company in its early stages.

You might be wondering how you go about building a reputation. I think it would be good to first consider that a reputation is something that is always in question, and there isn't necessarily an end destination. It's not a short-term solution; it requires multiple years of hard work and dedication to our craft. Sadly, in our modern world of social media and 24/7 news coverage, one bad decision or action could result in life-altering consequences.

Now, assuming you're in agreement that a reputation is constantly being built and developed, it's a wise idea to start thinking about the daily situations we experience that can contribute to a strong reputation.

Let's start with communication, one of the absolute fundamentals required in recruitment. We should be consistent with our communication in terms of providing updates when we've agreed; honest about the difficulty of a situation when it's not going as expected; and most important of all, we should keep our promises and do exactly what we said we would do. If we promise a candidate that we'll have feedback on their CV within five days, then we should provide exactly that.

Be personable. I'm not talking about asking how the weather is or did they have a nice weekend, but deeper and more meaningful questions. Remember names, even nicknames, or their kids' names, and what they get up to in their spare time. Do not underestimate the power in small differences like, 'How was your holiday? Where did you go again?' compared to 'Did you enjoy your week away in Santorini? I noticed the weather was nearly forty degrees over there.' The second is far more personable and will forge stronger relationships.

The single most important means to a prolonged respectable reputation in our industry is genuine achievements. When it's our first time working with a client, if we can accomplish a

Strengthen Your Reputation and Protect It at All Costs | 111

five-day turnaround to receive candidate profiles, so they're able to make an offer within three weeks, we'll gain respect and admiration, and it's highly likely we'll work with that client again. As for our colleagues, if we're able to bring on new clients every month, we will soon enjoy a reputation with those around us as someone who is motivated and good at our job.

So, to summarise, there's good news and bad news. The good news is that there are an endless number of ways to build our reputation. The bad news is there are an equally large number of ways that we can damage or lose our reputation. It's important to remember that every new vacancy we take on, every new interaction we have with a candidate, and every meeting we attend with our manager or senior leadership team is a chance not just to meet expectations but exceed them. All the promises we make are there to be followed through on. We live in a world where people like to talk about their experiences, so let's make sure we leave people feeling positive about their interactions with us. Who knows who they might tell.

Tip Twenty-Six
Hold Yourself Accountable to Everything

*'Accountability is a statement of personal promise,
both to yourself and to the people around you,
to deliver specific defined results.'*
Brian Dive, British consultant, author and speaker

Have you ever heard the story about Everybody, Somebody, Anybody and Nobody? It's a short story, more like a paragraph actually. To summarise, the ending of the story reads something like, 'It ended up that Everybody blamed Somebody when Nobody did what Anybody could have done'. This short story sums up what accountability, or rather, a lack of accountability looks like: passing the buck and playing the blame game.

Recruitment is a rewarding but challenging industry, and its challenges and disappointments are amplified unless we are accountable for our actions, behaviours and inputs. Some people confuse accountability with responsibility. Responsibility is typically task-oriented. For example, if five people

Hold Yourself Accountable to Everything | 113

are working on a project, and each is assigned one task, there is an expectation that they will complete that task to the best of their ability. Accountability goes one step further, and is better described as results-focused. When you are accountable, not only are you responsible for completing your task, but for the success of the overall project.

Working in recruitment will present us with hundreds of opportunities in any given month to either step up and become accountable or to fall into the trap of passing blame and denying liability. What is important, both for our personal growth and for our reputation with our colleagues, is that we become accountable for everything we do, the big and the small things.

Accountability starts with accepting that everything is within our control. You might be thinking, 'Huh, that's not right, Kieran. We are but homo sapiens flying through the solar system on an astronomical object playing out the universe's algorithm. How can we control everything?' And, well, you might have a point there. But when I talk about things being in our control, I mean those things we do and the decisions we make: these *are* in our control, always.

Bob Proctor once famously said, 'Accountability is the glue that ties commitment to the result.' I want to expand on the word commitment for a moment. I would like to think that most people reading this, and most in the recruitment industry as a whole, are committed to achieving their goals. We can think of commitment as desire to achieve, dedication to a cause and determination to achieve an outcome. But what about when we don't get that desired outcome? Or achieve that specific goal? That right there is where our true persona will show. Will we look externally and blame market conditions, the company's hiring process or bad luck, or do we focus internally on where we can get better next time?

There are probably too many scenarios to name where we can showcase our accountability, but let's cover a few that will be most common in the industry.

When we are dealing with clients, we become accountable for delivering a service and providing them with an individual(s) that they are looking for. If we decide to take on the vacancy with agreed criteria such as salary, location and benefits package, and assure the hiring manager we'll have three candidate profiles within five working days, we're not only responsible for those expectations, but we're being held accountable, both by them and, hopefully, ourselves. How about when a client's interview process is taking considerably longer than it should, and as a team we risk losing out on the best talent? First thoughts could be to blame the client (and rightly so) but are we doing everything in our power to adjust and influence the process? Again, it's a fact that sometimes we can't change or get the results we want, but by becoming accountable to the role we play in certain situations, we increase our chances.

I've been fortunate enough to manage several teams in different businesses before setting up my own recruitment agency, and there is one thing I've noticed from high performers: just how much they hold themselves accountable to their own goals and targets. Being accountable to our own goals and personal success not only supports us on our journey of personal growth, but it also supports our managers in how they can effectively manage us. If you haven't yet had the opportunity to manage a team – and if you've decided to read this book, you strike me as the type of

Hold Yourself Accountable to Everything | 115

person who will one day – then I'll share something brutally honest with you: people who don't hold themselves accountable are incredibly difficult to manage. It's always the market's fault, the client's issue for being slow, the competition for their dirty tactics, or the bus that turned up late.

To achieve any amount of success in recruitment, and stay at that level consistently, requires accountability for our actions. Both the good and the bad. True accountability over time effectively teaches the value of hard work, because we have no one else to blame but ourselves.

Tip Twenty-Seven
Talk Less, Listen More

'I remind myself every morning: nothing I say this day will teach me anything. So if I'm going to learn, I must do it by listening.'
Larry King, American author and radio host

I think it's only natural that anyone working in, or considering entering, the recruitment industry enjoys talking. Recruitment is essentially a sales role, and heavily phone-based, so you need some degree of confidence. I think it's fair to say a big proportion (though not all) of the industry have extroverted tendencies. But with confidence and extroversion occasionally comes (again, not always) inflated egos, and what's everyone's favourite topic to talk about? Themselves.

One of, if not the most important area of effective communication is active listening. I'd like to start by sharing some mind-boggling statistics. For those of you who would like to access the following information yourself, it's from an article published by WordsRated on November 28th 2023, titled 'Listening Statistics'.

Talk Less, Listen More | 117

Did you know that, on average, 4% of a person's time awake is engaged in some kind of listening activity? Did you also know that, if you haven't developed your listening skills, then you're likely to only be able to retain 50% of a conversation immediately after it's happened? Are you aware that active listening is identified by 64% of HR professionals as the most critical leadership skill?

If we're being honest with each other, you probably talk way more than you need to: in conversations with friends, colleagues and, most importantly, hiring managers or candidates. I have been a victim of verbal diarrhoea myself, in the early years of my recruitment career. It often feels like a necessity to fill gaps in conversations, oversharing information in the hope of convincing someone, or mindlessly talking because you may be nervous. Most of the time it comes down to a lack of confidence or knowledge of what we're talking about.

A golden metric that lives rent-free in my mind is to speak around 20% of the time and to let the other party have the other 80% of the conversation. The 20/80 rule is widely recognised from the Paretos Principle, which was first formulated all the way back in 1897. However, Mark Wayshak took Pareto's Principle and applied it to the art of communication, explaining that listening 80% of the time will allow you to ask deeper questions, and to repeat words and phrases back to the speaker, which results in a stronger bond.

Where can we apply these principles in the world of recruitment? The two most obvious areas are when speaking to candidates, or existing or prospective clients. Candidates are essentially our clients too, meaning we are here to serve, support and encourage them on their own individual journey toward finding an exciting career opportunity. Candidates are just like you and me: they want to be heard, and they like to feel special, too.

After all, it's *their* job search, *their* family that's feeling the effects, and *their* time that's being invested in an interview process. We covered earlier in this book that open-ended questions require the person answering to expand on their answer. Asking questions like 'What's your dream role?' or 'How does this role compare to the other places you're interviewed at?' will allow the candidate to construct answers that provide you with information that will help you with your search.

In fact, this 'dream role' question is one of my favourites. I think it's good practice to ask every candidate to share this with us recruiters. Allow them to verbally paint a picture of what would be above and beyond their expectations. Most importantly, inspire and motivate them to chase that dream, no matter how big, or small, it may be.

That said, do remember that, in recruitment, sadly, the principle that 'the candidate is always right' just isn't true. We recruiters are professionals. We get paid like professionals and our clients and candidates want us to act like consultants and advise where we can; whether they make it obvious or not, they do. We should be equipped with more knowledge than our clients when it comes to such things as realistic salary expectations and required skills. And when a client is being unrealistic, it's on us to share the truth of the situation.

When it comes to speaking with hiring managers, for some unknown psychological reasons, more often than not we recruiters put them on some pedestal. Unnecessary nerves or anxiousness leads to babbling, a style of communication that will have you speaking 80%, rather than 20%, of the time. Recruiters who aren't confident in asking the right questions, or don't have expertise in the area they're talking about, often find themselves talking in circles, fluffing up answers in the hope of sounding like they have some sort of idea.

This is made worse by the fact that hiring managers, whether they realise it or not, have a funny habit of not sharing essential information. Thus, when we have the opportunity to engage in a call where the purpose is to qualify and understand the role, it's imperative to allow the hiring manager a chance to speak openly by asking the right questions. Failure to follow the 20/80 rule when speaking to hiring managers will undeniably set you up for failure, because the information you'll have gained won't be sufficient to complete your job to the standard required. Through continuous learning, if you can evolve your listening to a level where your intentions are to *understand* rather than *simply to reply,* you'll be well on your way to becoming a top performer in your industry.

Tip Twenty-Eight
Don't Just Deliver, Trial Close

'The more that you understand, the more you can control.'
Virginia Satir, American author and psychotherapist

Humans have a natural tendency to become excited when sharing positive news. Think about some of your past experiences: passing your driving test for the first time, getting into that college you didn't think you would, telling your friends you're going on that holiday, or making your biggest placement to date. All of these milestones make us feel some type of way, so it's only right that we want to tell people about them as soon as we get the chance.

You could say we share the same feelings of excitement when we have positive news for other people, too: revealing to a partner you've booked some tickets to see their favourite band, or letting a candidate know they've received that job offer they so eagerly wanted.

Our intentions when sharing good news, both our own and for the benefit of someone else, are almost always to provide

Don't Just Deliver, Trial Close | 121

a joyous feeling. Sometimes we want people to recognise our achievements, boost our confidence and let us know we're doing a good job. Often we want to reduce others' anxiety or stress, and strengthen our relationships with them, too.

But high-level recruitment is a game of the minds. A game where most of the players are looking out for themselves first, and rightly so. In life, some people are out to deceive others, and it's no different in the world of recruitment. Candidates and clients will often withhold critical information for their own benefit, occasionally on purpose but more often than not because they do not think that piece of information is important. It usually is, however.

In recruitment, there is no greater battle of the minds than when it comes to delivering an offer. The decision to accept a new job is monumental, one of those sliding doors moments that could change the trajectory of your life. In most cases, it's naive to think that anyone would accept a new job opportunity on the spot. I mean, it happens, but it's rare.

In recent years, it's become almost guaranteed that candidates will be interviewing at multiple companies, carefully deciding who they like, who would be the best fit for them, and who can support their career goals. For a long time the people doing the hiring were in the driving seat. But fast forward to 2024, the times have changed, and the rules of recruiting have changed with them. There are times when the candidates interviewing have three or more offers to choose from already. *They're* in control, not us.

Once we accept that candidates are looking out for themselves, we can understand that whoever holds the most information in a negotiation will usually end up in the better position. I would like to share a few tips around delivering an offer that, over the years, have been paramount to landing some of my most important deals.

First and foremost is the trial close. For me, it's a non-negotiable. Usually completed after a final stage interview, a trial close is a series of specific, sometimes hypothetical questions to understand where the other party's at. 'How would you feel if you got an offer today?' or 'Who else do you need to speak to help make your decision?' or 'Are you in a position to accept today?' – these questions give you indications regarding how likely you are to make the placement.

Going one step further, we need to arrive at a figure that the candidate absolutely would accept, and establish the cut-off point below which they absolutely wouldn't. 'Knowing we shared your profile at the £65,000 mark, would you still accept at £65,000?' Interestingly enough, you'll often get mixed responses here. Some people will say yes, happily; others for whatever reason may now be expecting more; in rare instances some would even accept less because of the opportunity. Regardless of the answer, we then need to explore every other scenario. 'What would happen if they offer £63,000?' They may reply that they'd need to think it through. 'Ok, how about if they offered £61,000?' Here's where you'll likely get a reply along the lines of 'No, that's too low. I would have to decline'.

The primary goal here is to understand exactly what's needed to make the deal happen, so that we can truly work on behalf of the candidate. Equipped with this information, rather than making multiple calls back and forth, you can now tell the client that their offer of £61,000 is a non-starter, and that they'll need to increase.

Don't Just Deliver, Trial Close | 123

Sometimes, we recruiters are exposed to a phrase that sends shivers down our spines. It's like the word 'Voldermort' in Harry Potter. That word is 'counteroffer', and it's in our best interests to mitigate the risks of one from the very beginning of our engaging with a candidate. It may surprise you to learn that I talk about a counteroffer on the very first call with a candidate. It's the only way to know where you really stand. Have they spoken to their manager about the problems that are causing them to seek new employment? Have they asked for a salary raise? Often the answer to these questions will be no, which leaves me wondering if their job search is serious. And even if it is, what about when we do get an external offer? Now the client has some leverage, is it likely they will simply approach their current employer?

Some candidates will openly tell you that they may entertain a counteroffer, depending on what it is, and some will say the problems are deep-rooted and not financial, but we all know there's still a chance. The possibility of a counteroffer should be discussed at every interview stage, although not necessarily directly; often, the subject can be disguised. Simple questions like 'What's changed with your situation since we last spoke?' prompt an open response and test the candidate's temperature. Providing our opening call has gathered the right information about their problems and desires, we can relay these back to them throughout the process, to ensure they are making the right decision in looking for a new role. I always expect every person I'm representing to receive a counteroffer, which helps me reduce the risk from the very beginning.

Finally, a personal favourite (probably because I've been burned several times in the past here) is delivering our offer last. Let's imagine that a candidate has three final-stage interviews in a week. Ours is first, on a Tuesday, followed by two others on Wednesday and Thursday. If we can get an offer on Tuesday, and I've trial closed, run all the hypothetical scenarios by them and know, for a fact, they will not accept the offer until they've finished the interview process, it's in our best interest to withhold the offer. You may question this, but think about it: at this stage, the only piece of information we have is the offer, and if we give that away freely, there's a high chance it will be used as leverage to receive a higher offer elsewhere. It's happened to me, and I've seen it happen to my team colleagues. At a stage like this, it takes an admirable amount of self-discipline and mental strength to withhold the information and continue to work with the candidate to find out which opportunity suits them best, but it ensures you stay in the running, and all your hard work doesn't end up as simply a negotiation tool.

Although it can feel difficult to contain our excitement, and we often want to verbally explode and share our good news with a candidate, it's not the wisest thing to do. 'The more you understand, the more you can control': wait until you understand the entire picture, then you'll know how best to play your hand. Delivering an offer is one of the finest arts in recruitment and should be handled with care.

Tip Twenty-Nine
Be Caring and Kind

'You really can change the world if you care enough.'
Marian Wright Edelman, former president of
the Children's Defence Fund

When you read the title of this tip, who did you picture being caring and kind *to*? Was it the candidates you represent? Your colleagues? How about the cleaner or receptionist? Whilst the answers will vary, I have an inkling that most of you did not picture being caring and kind to yourselves. But to really be the best recruiter you can be, the answer should really be 'all of the above'.

The ability to be kind and caring is essential for all walks of life, but especially important in the recruitment industry. Caring is listening to truly understand someone's situation, or the problems they may be experiencing. Caring is putting yourself in somebody else's shoes and being attentive to their needs when they need it most. Caring is offering help, support or guidance when there is no direct benefit to yourself, and showing genuine sympathy in times of need.

Kindness, both with words and acts, undoubtedly has the power to make the world a better and happier place for everyone. The awareness to offer a helping hand when needed can improve our relationships with anyone. And kindness can be contagious. The benefits of kindness shown to other people return to benefit ourselves. Sometimes these benefits are material, sure, but sometimes they are as simple – and fundamental – as boosting our serotonin levels, amplifying our mood and reducing anxiety.

Recruitment is a bumpy ride of ever-changing circumstances and emotions. There will be times candidates don't turn up for an interview. Our initial reactions might be anger, disappointment, maybe even resentment. But we must approach the candidate with an open mind and open heart, and allow them an opportunity to expound on their situation. They may have experienced a family bereavement, an unprecedented circumstance or even an illness which has left them bedbound. Us recruiters come with built-in sceptical radars, and whilst some candidates may decide to bend the truth, we should never allow our emotions to get the best of us. We should always strive towards sympathy and understanding.

Our industry is built on relationships, and the recruiters with the strongest relationships will not only survive but thrive, even in market downturns. It's strikingly counterintuitive when some recruiters jeopardise a potentially extensive candidate relationship due to something so simple and relatable as life getting the way.

There will be many times when our colleagues may be struggling, too: struggling in their career, making placements or meeting targets; or struggling outside of work with personal

Be Caring and Kind | 127

situations or maybe even an illness. Our colleagues, just like us, live abstruse lives filled with ups and downs. And similarly to us, they may not feel comfortable sharing challenges in their personal lives with the people they work with. You will sometimes notice agitation when speaking to them, a constant pessimistic outlook or regular lateness and underperformance. It's like the tip of the iceberg theory: these people might have all sorts of things going on underneath the surface that we are not aware of. So we should treat them with kindness and support at all times.

The recruitment world is filled with excitement, but it can also be ruthless at times. Regardless of how our day or week may be going, it is of no benefit to anyone if we choose to be grumpy, greedy and unkind to others and ourselves.

You may be familiar with the saying 'You can't pour from an empty cup'; it's a paraphrase of a longer quote, but it gets across how we cannot support others if we don't care for ourselves first. How you take care of yourself will be different to how I take care of myself, and likely how others take care of themselves, too. But there are a few common areas that I hope we can all agree need regular investments, and those are the four core pillars of health - physical, mental, social and spiritual – that I reference regularly throughout this book. For a successful, prosperous recruitment career, and a happy life for that matter, it's vital we take care of ourselves on a daily basis. The world of recruitment can eat you up and spit you straight back out, but only if we let it.

At the beginning of this tip, I shared the words caring and kindness, but I'd also like to bring to light compassion, empathy, thoughtfulness and sympathy. When you think of these words, are your first thoughts about expressing them externally? About showing these qualities to other people? I think that hustle culture has some of us thinking that being kinder to ourselves is some kind of weakness, something that will hold us back. Not hitting targets? Work harder and longer hours. Falling ill and feeling under the weather? Pull your socks up and get on with it. A candidate drops out after accepting an offer? It's your fault, you should have done your job.

When someone else finds themselves in these scenarios, we will often show sympathy and concern, and encourage them to take some rest to recover. So why don't we take our own advice and be kinder to ourselves? There is a real unbalance in the way we treat ourselves compared to our colleagues.

Sometimes a working week in recruitment can feel like being in a boxing ring with Mike Tyson in his prime, taking hit after hit after hit, not knowing when you'll catch a break. It's inevitable that you'll be on the receiving end of some great wins, but undoubtedly even more losses. That's the unwritten contract we signed up for when committing to the recruitment industry. Some may seem insignificant in the grand scheme of things, but some will feel cataclysmic, leaving us unsure if we'll be able to recover. But when the going gets tough, that's when true character shows. It's in these times where we need to choose our words and actions, carefully.

Those things that we tell ourselves at the end of a tough working day make a difference. Things like 'It's just not good enough' or 'I can't do this anymore, I hate recruitment' aren't supporting you on your journey. Even if they hold some truth, we can still flip the negative self-talk into a more positive, encouraging tone. To get the best out of yourself, your colleagues, your staff and your clients, lead with the desire to genuinely care and watch your results change for the better.

Tip Thirty
Be Humble with Your Victories and Gracious in Your Defeats

'True humility is intelligent self-respect which keeps us from thinking too highly or too meanly of ourselves.'
Ralph W. Sockman, American pastor

'When we're winning, we're not as good as we think we are. When we're losing, we're not as bad as we think we are.' These incredibly humbling words are from the late Joe Paterno. If you're not familiar with Joe, sadly he passed away in 2012, but in his time he was a major league college football coach in the USA. And not just your average coach, but the most victorious coach in NCAA FBS history, winning twenty-four out of thirty-seven Super Bowl games.

If you've worked in recruitment for longer than six months, you'll know the truth of Joe's words: it's a rollercoaster, sometimes a rollercoaster on which you have forgotten to put your safety belt on; and like any rollercoaster, it's filled with ups and downs. But I think the unpredictability is what keeps people invested in the game. The adrenaline of signing new terms of business or making a placement is nothing short of an addiction. It's a euphoric feeling that we are constantly chasing.

Which brings us to the point of this tip: developing the ability of becoming humble both in victory and defeat. Both are difficult, taking a lot of personal strength, but they're crucial skills to master. In particular, I feel that remaining humble in victory is somewhere a lot of recruiters fall down, and in the worst instances, it could result in their professional demise.

There's no doubt that recruitment is a demanding profession, and we all work so incredibly hard to achieve our targets and support people into their dream roles. And there's times when all that hard work seems to pay off: when we feel on the top of our game, making multiple placements per month, bringing on new business on a weekly basis whilst regularly attending networking events. At such times, we might feel untouchable.

But when we're on these untouchable streaks we should remember just how quickly things can change. It's only right we embrace the rewards of our success, but as we do so, we should keep in mind: we're not as good as we think we are when things are going well.

Think about a few scenarios with me: almost all of us recruiters offer a rebate period; I've seen some completely unrealistic ones in my time, but we'll average it out at eight weeks. What could feel like a record-breaking month, with your new personal best on the board, could soon turn into a professional nightmare: one candidate accepts a counteroffer and another drops out of their new role in week one, and suddenly

Be Humble with Your Victories and Gracious in Your Defeats

you're facing an embarrassing walk into the office having spent the last week gloating to your colleagues.

In life just as recruitment, the tables always turn. Whilst we may be the head honcho right now, chances are someone is already chasing us down. Markets can fluctuate, projects can fail, and personal situations derail our performance and results.

A lot of responsibility comes with being a winner, top biller or high performer, and something that often flies under the radar is our colleagues looking up to us, whether consciously or unconsciously. The small things matter a whole lot more when all eyes are on us. Having the self-awareness to understand that our time at the top may be temporary can keep our actions and our words humble and respectful.

In my opinion, there is only one thing more gracious than being humble in victory and that's being humble in defeat. It really does take a remarkable amount of self-respect and discipline to remain humble when things get real.

Despite the effort and attention to detail we put in, across a working week of recruitment a lot of things are out of our control. Ultimately, there are hundreds of micro situations that can go against us. There will be days when someone may not turn up for an interview. There will be days when people do turn up for interviews but flunk them. There will be days when we are expecting a deal to land and it turns out the company doesn't make an offer. There will be days when we find out we've been 'backdoored' and a company has hired an individual they rejected through us. The way we handle these circumstances has a direct correlation to how successful we're going to be, and how we'll be treated by others. There truly is a different level of admiration for someone who handles these losses like a true champion.

I have, and you may have as well, seen people who completely erupt when something miniscule doesn't go their way. A minor occurrence of a candidate not getting past the first stage interview can result in negative talk around the office for the rest of the day, the need to leave the desk and get some fresh air, a completely pessimistic view of the whole week ahead and, at worst, some physical violence like punching a table. Yes, I've seen it all. If you regularly react to failure like this, just know you aren't doing any favours for yourself and your colleagues. Succumbing to our emotions and expressing them verbally is no recipe for success.

Everyone experiences negative emotions when things don't go their way. But there is a huge difference between someone who allows these emotions to control them, expressing them externally without regard for the people around them, and someone who processes these emotions internally, choosing when and how to show the best reaction. We can't control what feelings arise from the situations we encounter in recruitment, but we can control how we let them affect our attitude. Accept, acknowledge and process those emotions, and understand that remaining gracious when we've lost, but also humble when we've won, are skillsets that are admired by everyone.

Tip Thirty-One
The Money Is in the Follow Up

'Persistence, persistence, persistence.
I'm surprised how few entrepreneurs follow up.'
Mark Suster, American businessman and investor

Cold outreach – where you contact, usually unexpectedly, someone who doesn't have any previous connection with your business or service – is often misunderstood in sales, but particularly in recruitment. Reaching out to prospective clients, potential candidates or possible future employees is interesting for two reasons: on the more optimistic side, there's the vastness of opportunities when you have something of value to offer; on the other hand there's the constant disappointment of thinking you may be onto someone or something, only to then not hear back after the initial conversation.

Let's first approach cold outreach with an optimistic mindset. Approaching people that have no experience with your business is the most effective way of maximising your pipeline and building your network. Unless we take that chance and push outside of our comfort zone, we have no idea of just how many opportunities we are truly missing. When it's time to find candidates for new jobs, cold outreach works wonders. With the right messaging, you can excite people and prompt a response within the first message. There really is no faster way to expose yourself to new opportunities and accelerate your career.

I'm a serial optimist. In recruitment, I think it's extremely beneficial (and in life for that matter). But we should still consider both the positive and the *not so* positive outcomes. Approaching people cold often means unsolicited messages, particularly at times the receiver may be busy. No matter how good our intentions are, no matter how much value we might be trying to add, there's a very good chance that most of our cold outreach will be unappreciated, rejected and even ignored. In some rare instances, some lovely people will actually attack us for this approach. If this is you, please don't. And if you're ever on the receiving end, some friendly advice: take a step back and analyse the situation, then reply respectfully. Nobody wins in this kind of argument. Just remind yourself that cold outreach is an essential part of the game of sales and life, and a technique that will be with us for the rest of time.

This leads us on to where the real money is made. Effective and consistent following up is what separates the great from the good: the winners who attack life and hunt down opportunities like a wild lion searching for its prey, and the runners up who take what they can get and leave things to chance or 'fate'.

Following up with multiple touch points is efficacious in achieving new business, but you might be surprised at just how little us recruiters do so. Did you know that 80% of sales require five touch points or more to close? Yet 44% of sales-

The Money Is in the Follow Up | 135

people and recruiters give up after just one follow up call. Or even more staggering: were you aware that a mere 3% of your market is actively buying your services at any given time, and only 2% of sales are made on the first contact? Those are some crazy numbers. It is unfathomable how many opportunities we recruiters miss by not remaining persistent, investing time and effort into following up with prospects effectively.

Imagine that you can make yourself 80% more likely to win new business simply by ensuring five or more touch points with potential business – for nothing more than a few phone calls, emails, video messages, texts, WhatsApps or letters. Really think about it: to put yourself in the top 20% of recruiters, you simply need to follow up a measly six times. Of course, depending on the size of the account or organization you're trying to do business with, the sales cycle length might vary. When you are dealing with companies on the smaller side, you may be lucky enough to experience a win in the first point of contact. Larger companies, which are commonly referred to as big tickets, might take six to eighteen months of effort. But over the course of your career, you'll find the general trend remains true: the more doors you knock on, the more that will be opened for you.

Following up is where the money is made. Period. You'll need to continually develop both your listening skills and your ability to ask the right questions, so you know the right time to get in contact. It's important to follow up when you have agreed to do so, on the right day and with the right information. But most importantly of all, remember the stats shared in this tip; then each no you encounter can be taken in your stride, knowing that it brings you one step closer to a yes.

Tip Thirty-Two
Aspire to Become a True Consultant

'As a consultant, if you don't specialise, then it's hard to get great at one thing. It's hard to attract your ideal customer because your message is as diffused as your offer.'
Rob Malec, American author and business consultant

Despite what most recruiters think, most of us aren't actually consultants. Although many of us are gifted with the consultant title from day one, this description really couldn't be further from the truth. To become a qualified lawyer you would need to study for six years before becoming a junior. To become a qualified accountant, you would need to study for four years, and then you're entering the market at entry level. How long do you think it takes to become a medical consultant in the public sector? On average seven years. Of course, there's no denying that the medical profession requires more knowledge than recruitment, because of the amount on the line, but you get the gist.

I mentioned in the introduction of this book that (I hope)

Aspire to Become a True Consultant | 137

the recruitment industry is well on its way to becoming a respected industry, up there with the likes of those sectors mentioned above. But we still have a long way to go. If other professions require individuals to study or navigate through a training period just to reach entry level, I think this is something we should emulate in recruitment. I'm not suggesting that anyone entering the recruitment profession should be required to study as such, but I do think it would be beneficial for schools, colleges and universities to have courses available. With such a low barrier to entry in recruitment, I think we could put some more respect on the consultant title.

By definition, a consultant is a person who provides professional or expert advice in a particular field of science or business to either an organisation or individual: someone who is truly invested in their professional field and has a desire to help and support businesses or individuals to improve systems and processes or to support growth. Through key skills such as relationship building and expert communication, consultants are usually able to suggest and implement best practices and alternative ways of doing things.

You might be thinking all of that sounds like the role of a recruiter, right? Arguably, yes, but only once we develop our skills and understanding of our market, which can take years.

In the early years of your recruitment career, most recruiters – myself included – don't have a scooby on when, what or how to consult a multimillion-pound-turnover company on their recruitment practices. The infancy of your career should be a time of failure, growth and understanding. It's when we can learn our trade on the tools, as they say, just like an apprenticeship (only entry-level recruiters get paid considerably more). There is no shame in being a student in any industry. So why not be a student of recruitment?

The difficulty with embracing this mindset is that many people don't want to deal with the student or junior. Think about it, if you go to the doctors with severe pain, who do you want to see, the junior who's just graduated or the doctor with forty years' experience? Likewise, if you want a lawyer for an important court case, you're undoubtedly going to want a senior lawyer, rather than a junior. This is why no one in recruitment hands out titles like 'Junior Recruiter' or 'Student Recruiter'; it instantly devalues our services, no matter how good we are. Often entry-level recruiters are given the title of consultant for smoke and mirrors, to create the perception they are consulting on best practice. Essentially, we're told to fake it until we make it.

Regardless of your job title, if you're in your first one-to-three years of your recruitment career, you're a student of the game. Obviously, that doesn't need to be advertised, but it would be wise to bear it in mind, and to treat your approach to work like you're studying. Studying what works when it comes to sales outreach, and what doesn't. Studying who does well in speaking to candidates in your industry, and who doesn't. Studying who's attending all the networking events, and why, and who isn't. A student mindset will allow you to learn more about yourself from others, and from your failures and successes.

The ultimate goal for any recruiter who takes their craft seriously is to be valued as a true consultant to his clients. As the infamous quote from Rob Malec explains, it's hard to become a truly great consultant unless you specialise. It would be unreasonable to expect yourself to become a consultant of the

Aspire to Become a True Consultant | 139

recruitment industry as a whole, although it is possible. For most of us, it is enough to become a consultant in a niche, somewhere you have developed a keen interest and understanding in, like software engineers that operate in the FinTech industry located in Belgium, or family lawyers in Kent, for example. See how hyper-focused these are? By creating a micro-niche, just imagine the knowledge you could pick up and utilise with clients. You'll know when you are truly at a consultant level, or at least on your way, when candidates and clients are asking for your advice and support. Candidates will lean on you for support with their CV, salary expectations and how realistic their career goals might be. Clients will leverage your knowledge on how long it might take to find a certain skillset, what they may need to pay for that skillset, and why they keep losing out on talent to the competition. When you get to this stage, recruitment is a truly rewarding and congenial industry to work in, and you will have truly earned the title of consultant.

Tip Thirty-Three
Proactivity Beats Reactivity, Every Time

'If you're proactive, you focus on preparing.
If you're reactive, you end up focusing on repairing.'
John C. Maxwell, American author and orator

If you study any top performer in your industry, I bet that proactivity is a trait they have in spades. Proactivity is self-initiated behaviour that endeavours to find solutions to problems before they occur. To be effectively proactive requires the ability to envision the future and focus on the things that we can control.

Reactivity, on the other hand, does have a place in recruitment, but relying on it too much will cause us stress and regular disappointment. When I hear the word 'reactive', I picture someone scrambling to catch up with events, rather than getting ahead of them. Google shares synonyms like 'complaining', 'finger pointing', 'showing anger' or 'fear of losing control'. None of those sound like they would benefit a high performing recruiter, do they?

Proactivity Beats Reactivity, Every Time | 141

It's incontestable that there will be parts of the recruitment lifecycle that will require us to have good reaction skills. Although we can plan for most things, sometimes recruitment is unpredictable: a candidate decides that an opportunity is not for them during a rebate period, or a hiring manager calls us with a contract vacancy with one day's notice. Our reactions, the speed at which we can comfortably deal with a situation, are of real value in times like this. That said, I would avow that most of our good work in recruitment can be done proactively.

Proactivity requires an upfront commitment of energy and mental capacity to plan, predict and prevent unwelcome situations or problems. It is an investment of resources into shaping conditions conducive to performing at a higher level and producing better results. It is categorically never going with the flow and assuming the best.

The most important area to be proactive is in our approach to speaking with candidates. As always in recruitment, there will be times when our job flow might not be where we would like it to be, or we might have a specific job for which we need to search for a certain skillset. The proactive approach of regularly speaking to candidates, without a job to present them, allows you to be one step ahead of the competition. We create our own luck in recruitment. Who knows where a conversation might take us? It could be a referral into someone else looking for work, or it could be three leads regarding where that candidate interviewed last week. We won't have anything for that candidate right there, but that's why we then ask permission to keep in touch because we frequently get opportunities in their space. I can't tell you how many times I have spoken to someone, had nothing for them, then two weeks later I've landed a new opportunity and suddenly had five people ready to reach back out to. That is the true definition of being proactive and productive.

When it comes to working with our clients, most of us will at times fall guilty of remaining on the back foot and waiting for vacancies as and when they get to us. That feeling of receiving a new vacancy to work on is second to none, but it's quickly followed by the feeling of anxiety because we didn't plan for the vacancy, we have no real pipeline of candidates, and time is most certainly against us.

Proactivity works just as well with clients as it does candidates. There are two main ways to increase our proactivity with clients, and the most obvious one is simply to ask. Let's have the confidence to ask our clients what their roadmap looks like for the next twelve months. Do they have any immediate hiring plans in the next three months? Are they expecting any projects that will need contract resources? Would they look to replace anyone that leaves the team in the next six months? Imagine you find out that your client has budgeted plans to hire four new individuals in three months' time. I know what I would be doing over the next two months, and that's making a talent pool of candidates that match that skillset, potentially even speaking to some to pre-empt their interest. That's proactivity in action.

Another way, and this is proactivity in its truest form, is not only understanding what vacancies you have worked previously, but figuring out what roles clients will most likely recruit for in the future – without them sharing that information with you. If a client has a very specific skillset in their engineering team, and you know, for a fact, they are interested in people with that skillset, you could be consistently searching for that

Proactivity Beats Reactivity, Every Time

profile whether there's a live vacancy to work or not. Over time, you will then have a pool of candidates built and ready to approach when that vacancy does go live. You might even have the confidence to approach your clients with a candidate who possesses their desired skillset even when there are no vacancies.

Proactivity is a mindset. It's constantly being in a state of optimism with a desire to move forward. And you'll have good reasons for your optimism, because the more proactive you are, the more success you'll run into. Two weeks of candidate calls with no career opportunity to present to them may seem like a never-ending task, but it all pays off when something lands and you're two weeks ahead of everyone else. Like I said: in recruitment we create our own luck. The more calls you make, the more questions you ask, the more work you put in when you're not required to, the more 'luck' you'll enjoy. As Oprah Winfrey once said, 'Luck is a matter of preparation meeting opportunity.' I think that sums it up perfectly.

Conclusion

And there we have it, thirty-three ways to become a better recruiter (and human being). There are undoubtedly many more ways, but these are the thirty-three I wish I had understood earlier on in my recruitment career. You may have noticed that most of the tips I have shared throughout this book aren't secrets, things that only the elite know and use. Rather, they're the core fundamentals of recruitment done to an expert standard. You see, the introduction of AI into our industry will bring some benefits, allowing us to improve in certain areas, but the fundamentals of recruitment – like human interaction and communication – should never be overlooked. I genuinely hope that you have enjoyed reading this book and leave with some value. I'm deeply invested in becoming the best recruiter I can be, and I hope I have inspired

Conclusion | 145

you to do the same. I leave you with these tips and hope you will join me on a journey of growth. It's over to you.

If you enjoyed this book, and most importantly have taken some value away, I encourage you to connect with me and to join me on my personal development journey, and so I can support you on yours.

As the Founder of Place Recruitment, we source talent in the technology markets across the UK and Europe. For anything social media related, the only platform you will find me on is LinkedIn. You can connect with me at **https://www.linkedin.com/in/kieranplace**

I always make time to support others, If you have any questions you think I might be able to help with, you can contact me directly at kieran@placerecruitment.uk

If you're already on the journey of becoming the best recruiter you can be (or plan to start after reading this book!), it would be well worth visiting my website, letting me know you've read the book and signing up to receive exclusive weekly content from my newsletter. You can sign up at www.kieranoconnor.co.uk

And finally, almost a decade of information has been poured into this book altruistically to support you. Can I ask, if you have taken value from this book, could you promise me three things? Firstly, tell a friend, to tell a friend. Encourage your colleagues to pick up this book, too. Secondly, please share your feedback with me publicly on LinkedIn, I'll be sure to comment back. And finally, and most importantly, I would appreciate it if you could leave me an Amazon review. It will help more than you ever know.

Thank you and good luck.